THE
PROPERTY
TRIANGLE

How to
source, value, purchase
and profit from property.

GRAHAM KINNEAR

BSc(Hons), FPCS, CPEA, CRLM, MGIS, FPC, MLIA(Dip), CeMAP, DipDEA

COPYRIGHT

This book is copyright material and must not be copied, reproduced, transferred, distributed, leased, licenced or used in any way except as specifically permitted in writing by the publishers as allowed under the terms and conditions under which it was purchased or as strictly permitted by applicable copyright law.

Any unauthorised distribution or use of this text may be a direct infringement of the author's and publisher's rights and those responsible may be liable in law.

The right of Graham Wilson Kinnear to be identified as author of this work has been asserted to him in accordance with the Copyright, Designs and Patents Act 1988.

ISBN: 978-1-326-18096-6

DISCLAIMER

Please note that the material contained in this book is set out in good faith for general guidance and no liability can be accepted for loss or expense incurred as a result of relying in particular circumstances on statements made in this book. The laws and regulations are complex and liable to change and readers should check the current position with the relevant authorities before making any personal commercial arrangements. This book does not seek to provide any specific legal or financial advice nor should it be treated as such. Readers are strongly advised to seek professional advice prior to dealing in property.

DEDICATION

In memory of my wonderful father Iain Wilson Kinnear.

The finest inspiration a boy could have.

THANKS

Initially I would like to extend my thanks to the two ladies in my life.

My partner Vyckie for her tireless efforts in assisting me with this book, for her constructive comments (and some not so constructive!), encouragement and relentless proof reading. This in addition to her love and unfailing ability to make me smile.

Enormous thanks also to my Mum, Joan Kinnear, for her lifelong interest and encouragement in all that I do and all that I set out to achieve.

And to my son Ben, the pleasure, pride and purpose that I derive from being part of your life, watching you grow up and develop is immeasurable.

I thank you from the bottom of my heart, I love you all. My journey in life would be far more challenging, far less fun and with far less purpose without you.

ACKNOWLEDGEMENTS

Thanks to Mrs Leah Goodburn for the design of the front cover, spine and rear cover of this book.

Thanks also to my publisher for all their assistance in extracting this book from my head and into print!

ABOUT THE AUTHOR

Graham Wilson Kinnear
BSc (Hons), FPCS, CPEA, CRLM, MGIS, CeMAP, FPC, MLIA (Dip), DipDEA.

Graham Kinnear was born in Leeds in 1974 and educated at Eltham College, London SE9. Following his A Levels he attended DeMontfort University from where he graduated with a BSc (Hons.) degree in Land Management in 1995. His final year thesis was entitled *"The factors that affect the residential property market"* and the research undertaken for that project was the perfect education for a future property investor.

Upon leaving University, Kinnear was keen to increase his level of knowledge and qualifications in order that he could accelerate his career in property. As a result he subsequently obtained the Certificate of Practice in Estate Agency, Certificate in Residential Lettings and Management, became Fellow of the Property Consultants Society, Associate of the Architecture and Surveying Institute and the Guild of Incorporated Surveyors. Whilst acting as an agent for Clients he was also a Fellow of the Association of Residential Letting Agents and a Fellow of the National Association of Estate Agents where he was exempted from the admission exam in view of his considerable qualifications. In addition he qualified as a financial advisor.

This thirst for knowledge has not diminished and accordingly when the legislation was introduced for Energy Performance Certificates, Kinnear promptly qualified as a Domestic Energy Surveyor too!

Kinnear joined the Alliance and Leicester Property Services in July 1995 as a Graduate Trainee and purchased his first property in December 1995 at the tender age of 21.

In terms of credentials for property investment, Kinnear is certainly a voice that is heard in the Industry. Engaged initially as a trainee in 1995, he had, within 5 years, reached the level of Senior Branch Manager with one of the nations largest corporate estate agency chains and had taken a cold start office to number 1 office in its first year.

He also gained experience with Black Horse Agencies in Maidstone, Halifax Property Services in Canterbury and Broadstairs as well as two independent firms, Cockburn in South London and Homes.Com where he was Manager and Financial Advisor responsible for the offices at Borough Green, Heathfield and Uckfield. During this period he undertook a variety of roles including Senior Negotiator, Branch Manager, Senior Manager and Trainer.

Graham was incredibly lucky to have the opportunity to work with some of the real success stories of the industry including Rob Tucker, Simon Dunand and Ian Browne.

With such a broad range of experience and seemingly endless determination he decided to set up his own practice with two colleagues in 2003. This expanded to four branch offices and received no less than 8 National Awards including a Bronze award for Best UK Letting Agent at the Sunday Times National Awards.

Furthermore in 2007 he launched a firm, with a colleague, which advises landlords on the issues that they face with their property investments. This firm has also gone from strength to strength and has also been acknowledged at a national level. The firm has been finalist three times in the category of Legal Supplier at the Landlord and Buy to Let Awards as well as being a shortlisted finalist at both the Property Drum Awards and the coveted ESTAS.

It was therefore no surprise that in 2008 Kinnear was possibly the youngest ever finalist in the "Lifetime Achievement in Property" at a National Awards Event, being beaten to the award by Harry Hill, the former Chairman of Countrywide. Graham is also featured in the "Who's Who" Book of British Business Elite. He has and continues to contribute to property related matters on television, radio and has had over 2000 property related articles published in printed media.

He has over the years devised and developed a proven method through which others can succeed in property investment.

He has been involved as a purchaser or JV partner in the purchase of around 150 residential and commercial properties in the UK and provides advice to Clients on their property investment plans. His purchases have included everything from flats, houses, shops, bars and even a pier! One of his joint venture purchases won a Town Pride Award for its restoration work to a listed building.

Kinnear runs the Landlords Clinic for the London Landlord Property Meet and regularly writes for local and regional media on property issues.

He continues to invest in property, acts for Clients on a consultancy basis as well as speaking at a number of landlord and investor events around the Country.

We can now add to his biography that he is also a published author specialising in the property sector!

Kinnear lives in Margate on the East Kent coast with his partner Vyckie, son Ben, an aged cat and Bruce the springer spaniel.

CONTENTS

INTRODUCTION

In the business world, everyone is paid in two coins; cash and experience. Take the experience first; the cash will come later.
Harold Green

This book is not designed to be a 'get rich quick' scheme nor is it intended to replace the education and knowledge that can be gained through undertaking property related academic courses and/or practical experience.

If you are looking for a book which promises you the ability to buy hundreds of properties without putting any money down or the ability to earn thousands each month without even owning a property then regrettably you have made the wrong choice.

If however you want to know some of the secrets of a proven property investor and to adopt the methods he uses to ensure that every property purchased is a good investment then this is possibly the best book you could have chosen! If you are an Estate or Letting Agent or indeed a Surveyor, then I hope that you will find this book equally useful in providing useful and accurate advice to your Clients.

What is intended is that the novice investor can understand how property investment works and make informed decisions without vast experience to ensure that their investments work, the prices they pay are competitive and that the return they get meets their expectations. Simply on the basis of one property purchase this knowledge will justify the purchase price of this book many times over!

1

In addition to providing you with what I believe to be the fastest and most effective way of calculating what you should pay for an investment property, I aim to guide you through the process so that you have a greater understanding of what is involved before you get in too deep! It may be upon reflection that you decide that property investment is not for you. If that is the case then at least this book will have allowed you to make an informed decision. I do however hope that you progress with your plans for property investment as it is possibly one of the most rewarding, exciting and interesting ways of earning a living. After 20 years in property I still get a real "buzz" when I buy an investment property.

Before we begin you should understand that Buy to Let property is a medium to long term strategy and so if you are looking for a big fast buck then perhaps you will need to reconsider your goals and look at property trading or development. These will be touched upon in this book although the focus of the following chapters is principally in respect of Buy to Let.

Initially, it is important to understand that the property market is a market like any other. Prices change as a result of supply and demand. The level of supply and demand is impacted by a number of factors such as government policy, interest rates, consumer behaviour, inflation and confidence to name but a few.

As with all marketplaces there can be winners and losers however, as with all marketplaces, the ones who succeed are generally the ones who approach matters in a structured fashion, are equipped with a degree of knowledge and who make prudent decisions. My aim is to equip you for market success!

In order to do so I am going to share with you the model I use which takes account of the issues that impact the market and is one which can be understood by anyone. It can be used for any residential investment property, anywhere in the UK and I truly believe the method works. I call it "The Property Triangle." We shall discuss it in greater detail in Chapter 4.

So insightful is this model that a number of people were surprised at my book on the basis that why would I want to give out the secrets of property investment that I have acquired over the last 20 years and to help others that may come and operate in my marketplace?

Well quite simply there are several million properties in the UK and even with some additional investors enthused following the reading of these pages, this will not impact my ability to find a property to buy.

Furthermore I think that property investment is key to the private rented sector and housing is key to the economy. If investors get it wrong it creates an economic problem and they will not do it again. If, hopefully as a result of reading my book, they get it right they will be encouraged to do it again and they will benefit, their families will benefit and the economy at large will benefit. Whilst it is possibly ambitious to suggest that my ideas on their own could create nationwide economic growth, as one retailer says "Every Little Helps!"

Aside from that, there is a big part of me that wants to give something back, to allow people to benefit from my knowledge and experience and to help those who want to listen.

I think I have been incredibly lucky in my property career. I have had great mentors, some great opportunities and derived enormous satisfaction from working in property. I hope that your journey can be as enjoyable and rewarding.

Many people in Britain have an interest in property and you will need to have such an interest in order to willfully dedicate your time and efforts in creating a property portfolio and the benefits that can bring.

Do remember that this should be an enjoyable and rewarding feeling; you are trying to create a passive income, which will allow you to supplement or even replace the salary of your existing job.

As someone once said to me "Spend a few years doing what others are not prepared to do and spend the rest of your life doing what others have not got the time to do."

So without further delay, let us start you on your journey...

CHAPTER ONE
WHY INVEST IN PROPERTY?

If you listen to your fears you will die never knowing what a great person you might have been.
Robert Shuller.

Residential Property has not always been such a popular investment medium as it is today. When I was growing up tenants were better protected by the Rent Acts than they are currently by the Housing Act and Buy to Let finance had yet to be thought of. Instead property investors would use commercial finance to purchase property as an investment. Alternatively there were investment funds that you could invest in which in turn invested directly in property although their investments were principally commercial property. Whilst I suppose that satisfied some investors, for me there is no substitute to the tangibility of owning your own property.

Aside from a certain clumsiness of the market, most people were conditioned to look at alternative investments. There was an established incentive for an individual to purchase a property for their own occupation but financial investment advice was more likely to take the form of national savings, annuities, pension contributions, stocks and shares or unit trusts rather than suggesting that you consider a second residential property as an investment.

The Housing Act changed all of that and in around 1995/1996 Buy to Let finance became available. From memory it was a venture involving some of the lending institutions and the Association of Residential Letting Agents. In short it meant that individuals could purchase a property to rent out as an investment and would pay something far more competitive for their finance than had previously been the case. Furthermore the legislation meant that tenants were no longer protected in the same way and so it was far easier for the owner to secure possession of the property in the event that they needed to sell. This reduced a lot of risk from the mortgage lenders point of view and meant that many competitive Buy to Let mortgage deals starting being offered in the market. Whether the explosion in Buy to Let was predictable at the time is unclear but the market has grown significantly and there are now reported to be almost 1.5M landlords in the UK.

Consequently, since around 1995, residential property has been an acknowledged and very popular investment medium. There are a number of valid reasons why property should, in my opinion, be a top priority for those serious about investment.

Over the years property values tend to increase at a rate greater than inflation. Money left in a deposit account will tend to lose value over a period of time due to the eroding effect of inflation. This is particularly important as without an inflation beating investment the spending power of your money reduces each year due to the effects of inflation. To give you an idea of the effects of inflation just think of how much you paid for a packet of crisps at your school tuck shop (In my case just 5p!) or have a look at how much a Ford Mondeo cost when they were launched 20 years ago. For this reason alone it is critical to have an investment that will outperform inflation as without it you will, at best, stand still or worse still be going backwards.

Secondly there are few other investment opportunities, which have two positive money streams. Firstly the property will yield an income via the rent it attracts and secondly it is hoped that the value of the property will increase over time. Adding these two facets together means it generally outperforms most other investments.

If you need convincing in this respect then have a look on the Internet to see how house prices have changed since the Second World War. Reports vary but there is a general acceptance that house prices double every seven to 12 years and whilst there have been some periods of recession in that time, the overall trend for house prices has been upwards. Additionally you may wish to look at how rents have increased over the last decade or two. Using my own experiences, rents have increased by approximately 100% in my area over the last 15 years. So you can have two returns, both of which can hedge you ahead of inflation.

A further attraction is the physical tangibility of a property which allows the owner to see it, feel it and touch it in a way that is generally not possible with other investments such as unit trusts and shares. This aspect of property is one which is doubtless a large contributor to its popularity. How many of you watch Homes under the Hammer and some of the other property investment programmes on the television? Would it be as interesting if it were "Annuities under the Hammer?" I think not!

Property has become far more popular as an alternative to a pension. Whilst it is possibly true to say that the tax treatment is less favourable for property than with a traditional retirement plan, it is also probably fair to say that a well selected property could yield in rent the same as an annuity without the owner having to sacrifice the initial purchase price as with an annuity the initial investment is lost on death, whilst a property can be left to someone else to benefit from. As an example you could use £100,000 to buy an annuity which would give you a monthly income for the rest of your life. Upon death that annuity ends and therefore your beneficiaries of your estate cannot benefit from it. An alternative many are looking at is that they instead buy a property for £100,000 and the rental income replaces what would have been their annuity income. When they die they can leave the property and any income it generates to their beneficiaries subject, of course, to any inheritance tax liabilities.

For those interested in gearing, property is also one of the very few assets that you can purchase using someone else's money! I will consider the use of finance in a little more detail in Chapter 3.

The other benefit for those of you contemplating property as a business is that you can almost predict the performance of the business before you invest any money into it. Once you have read and digested the content of this book you will be aware of the return you will get on your money and the income your property business will generate. How many cold start businesses can do that?

To give you an example of the potential of property, ask your parents how much they paid for their first home and then have a look on one of the internet portals and see how much that house would be now. In addition to that gain, add up the number of years rent that the property could have achieved and you will have a total income stream for that property. Compare that with any other investment medium over the same time period and see if anything can beat property. If you find something that provides a better return then please let me know!

To partially demonstrate this point I have just dug out the file on my own home and found an old conveyance in there dated 1956. At that time my house changed hands for the princely sum of £1,800. That is about the same price as I paid for my first car! Quite incredible when you think about it.

Aside from the above, the love affair and obsession with property in the UK appears to continue unabated despite the turbulent economic backdrop of recent years. Varying anecdotal reports exist that discussing property and house prices remain one of the most popular British conversations.

Not only do we as a nation seem to culturally aspire to owning property there are now growing numbers who aspire to own a portfolio of property. A recent survey suggests that more than half of the UKs landlords intend to increase their portfolio over the coming year. If you fall into this category then I hope that, contained within the following pages, there is something that assists you in your journey.

Why did I invest?

A lot of people that I meet who are involved in property started off by looking after a family property or a family portfolio and then from there they developed their own portfolio. My story is slightly different in that my parents never bought property for investment purposes.

My father trained as a quantity surveyor but eventually qualified as a Chartered Loss Adjuster. His job meant we would move home four times during my childhood and possibly as a result of that, we spent many a Saturday afternoon peering into Estate Agents windows. He was interested in property and I think that is what probably got me started.

From about the age of 12 I decided I wanted to be an estate agent primarily as I wanted to be able to value any property in any town. The idea of property investment had not yet come to me but I had and still have, a huge fascination with property.

When I owned my Estate Agency I always used to ask the question when I interviewed people *"Why do you want to become an Estate Agent?"* The most common answer was that they had an interest in property and looking at other people's homes. I even had a few say to me that they were attracted to agency, as Estate Agents always seemed to have nice cars.

Whilst, as a Porsche driver, I do have an interest in nice cars and clearly an obsession about property, my personal motivation for wanting to be an estate agent was solely that I wanted the ability to look at any house, anywhere in the Country and be able to accurately discern how much it was worth. This was to me a magical skill that I wanted to master.

Following my schooling at Eltham College in South London I undertook a surveying degree at University. I absolutely loved the course content and was incredibly eager to put my new knowledge to good use in the real world. As any graduate will admit and despite my Dad reminding me that *"You are no better a surveyor today than you were yesterday"* the day I graduated I thought I knew it all!

I was quickly brought back down to earth with my first posting following university, which was with the Estates Department of a Local Authority in Buckinghamshire. Keen to embrace the recently acquired skills of an enthusiastic surveying graduate they deemed it appropriate to enlist me to undertake a series of rating valuations on a range of public owned buildings, most notably public toilets!

I lasted just a few weeks before leaving in the hope that I could put my degree, endless enthusiasm and determination to greater use! My catalyst for leaving was that they asked me to!

My first "proper" post University job which didn't involve public toilets started in July 1995 with the Alliance and Leicester in Ashford, Kent. I am showing my age now, as they haven't had a property services division for almost 20 years now!

It was a great start for me and I had a very supportive management team above me. Ashford was just benefitting from a new international station and all sorts of redevelopment was planned for the town. It was a fun and vibrant place to work and house prices were starting to show some improvement following the early nineties recession. In addition Kent was a County with which I was already familiar.

At that stage I had not even considered Buy to Let as an investment medium. Whilst I was at University I was in Halls of Residence for the first year, in the second year I and three others rented a four bedroom detached property which the landlord was renting as his job had taken him abroad for a couple of years and in the third year I rented the home of someone who had gone to undertake voluntary work overseas for a year. So up until this point I had still never met a "landlord" not least as I have mentioned, whilst my parents undertook a number of financial investments such as shares, unit trusts and pension arrangements, they did not invest in property. To my knowledge nor did any of their friends.

I was initially given the job of Trainee although pleased that this title was omitted from my business cards! The work was interesting and I was involved in residential valuation and sales as well as getting some experience with development land and new build schemes.

One of the first accompanied viewings I undertook with the Alliance and Leicester was at a very tired three bedroom house at 31 Bond Road, Ashford, Kent. At £30,000 for a three bedroom Victorian home it seemed like the price was right!

I was tasked to show round a Mr. Winfield and I was determined to sell him the property, not only to impress my new employer but also to get my hands on my first commission cheque!

As we walked up to the property I was enquiring after his current property to try and establish whether he was reliant on the sale of that in order to proceed. Whilst he didn't directly answer my question he did tell me a little bit about his current home. His current house sounded delightful and I was hugely deflated as I opened the door to this tired property in need of renovation. How could he prefer this to his current house?

I was stunned when he asked me to submit an asking price offer on the house. Jubilant with my new found selling skills I headed back to the office and reported the news to my manager. It was only when I was then told that Mr. Winfield does indeed have a lovely house and does indeed have no intention of moving to Bond Road, that I realised I had met my first buy to let investor!

Mr. Winfield had a normal day job and he was also a property landlord. This to me seemed the perfect mix. His situation was even more perfect as he was a shop fitter by profession and therefore had all the necessary staff and skills to undertake the refurbishment of this property he wanted to buy.

It was mid August 1995 and my mind was made up. I would earn as much as I could in Estate Agency and use the money to invest in property. On that basis I would not need to contribute to a pension and eventually I could possibly have an income without having to go to work at all! To use the modern day moniker of "no brainer" this really was a light bulb moment in that you could have the rental income from the property and enjoy any capital growth. And on the face of it I could have lots of fun in the process!

After just four months in the job and four months of struggling on a basic salary of just £6,000, I managed to talk my manager into a pay rise and managed to buy a two bedroom property in Ashford for £38,250. Aside from the achievement of being able to be the first of my peer group to move out of home I also selected the property on the same estate as where my manager owned a buy to let investment. My reasoning was that when I could afford a bigger house I could keep this one in the knowledge that homes in this area rent out well.

This is typical of my approach, always looking to the future in terms of what I could do. I still own that property and it has been let to the same tenants for several years and provides me with a yield of 19% against what I paid for it. It is also now worth four times what I paid for it back in 1995. Thank you Mr. Winfield for the inspiration!

Whilst I am assured that it was nothing to do with my estate agency skills, regrettably the Alliance and Leicester decided to close their property division and so I was facing redundancy. I

13

therefore thought it prudent to put the bigger house plans on hold. Instead, I thought I would remain in my house and try and save for the deposit on an investment property. I purchased my first proper Buy to Let property in 1997. By that time I was working in Canterbury for Halifax Property Services and the market was really starting to move.

I agreed to purchase a two bedroom ex-council apartment just north of the City for £36,750 in the hope that I could get a rental of £400 a month (Oh how I wish it was still that easy to find deals with a 13% yield!!). I was one of the first customers to take advantage of the newly created Buy to Let funding with the Woolwich Building Society and whilst I cannot remember the mortgage rate, I recall making a little profit from the rental each month.

I still own this property today and its value is probably £150,000 and the rental income is now £850 a month. These figures show the number of people who have got involved with Buy to let and thereby driven yields down in some areas by 50%. That same property would just about yield an investor 7% now whereas if that had been the case in 1997 the property would have cost around £70,000!

Six months after I purchased this property I was given the opportunity to purchase an identical one in the same block for £43,000. I declined, thinking it was too expensive bearing in mind I had paid less than £37,000 six months earlier.

This is an error that many investors make and one that I still fall foul of today. You should not base your valuation and thoughts on historic data. The property was worth £43,000 and had I paid it and bought the property then it too would today be worth £150,000. If it had been on the market six months earlier it would have been £36,750 and if it was on the market today it would be £150,000. The advice I proffer is to buy sensibly at the most competitive level that you can. Do not walk away from a deal because you already own one in that street which you paid less for. It is an advantage to you that you paid less as it shows the market is moving in the right direction or that the area is improving and therefore your original investment decision was a correct one.

Someone once told me that the best time to buy is today. There is a lot of truth in this statement, given that, allowing for short-term peaks and troughs, house prices generally move up over time. The sooner you buy, potentially the greater gain you could have and clearly the more income you will generate.

I suppose the lesson here is *"Don't wait to buy property but instead buy property and wait."*

Please be reassured that it is not my intention to simply illustrate this book with examples of properties I have bought and the rents they achieve or the price that I managed on resale. Helpfully my goal is to try and educate you in terms of how to select a property, how to value it and how to maximize your experience as a property investor.

CHAPTER TWO
TYPES OF PROPERTY INVESTMENT.

Real estate investing, even on a very small scale, remains a tried and true means of building an individual's cash flow and wealth.
Robert Kiyosaki

The main aim of this book is to equip you to be a buy to let investor. My assumption is that you are wanting to acquire property which you will rent out to either enjoy an income on an ongoing basis or to realise capital growth upon resale. I am even alert to the fact that many of you may be seeking both! However for completeness and to give you some additional confidence in operating within the property environment you are about to immerse yourself in, I shall make mention of some of the other property investment opportunities in order that you can make your own decisions in terms of which may suit you best:

Ground Rent Investments:
The clue is in the name with ground rents. You are effectively buying the freehold, normally of a block of flats, where individual properties have been sold on long leases. You are therefore entitled to receive the ground rent which is payable to the landowner for the duration of the lease.

In addition to the ground rent you will be able to make a charge to the leaseholder in the event that the leaseholder wants an extension to their lease or a variance in its terms. As well as the income, you will be responsible for running the property, arranging insurance and the maintenance of the communal areas and grounds but you are normally able to recharge these costs to the leaseholders under the terms of the lease.

You can pick up ground rent investments for as little as £1,000. There is a readily tradable market for these type of investments and so resale is generally fairly straightforward.

I have bought several of these over the years, normally where I own one or more of the leasehold interests in the building. The ones I have purchased have been at around the £1,000 level and so with just one request for a lease extension and you have more than made your money back.

These types of investments are sometimes available through estate agencies but are more often placed into auctions.

Life Tenancies:
Life tenancy investments were once the preserve of the institutional investors but more recently have become available and enjoyed some appeal to private buyers. They offer an interesting alternative to a traditional Buy to Let investment.

In short they work on the basis that the owner of the property sells their property to an investor on the understanding that they can remain living there, rent free. The investor buys the property at a discount to its market value and their incentive is that upon the death of the owner, or them moving into full time residential care, the property will be vacant and the investor can sell it or rent it and realise an income in respect of rental or a capital gain in the event of sale.

It is normal that the occupier of the property maintains the insurance and maintenance for the property although investors should be clear that there is no rent payable during this period.

In my area a property which would be worth say £170,000 as a vacant property could change hands at around £75,000 on a life tenancy basis although clearly the prices depend on the ages of the occupiers.

Lease options:
Lease options are one of the more exotic or out of the box property investments that have gained some real popularity over recent years. The marketing spin was that they offered investors an opportunity to increase their portfolios even at a time when their banks may not have been willing to lend. The attraction to the seller is that the scheme will enable sellers to sell up and move on even if they are currently in negative equity.

The scheme works on the basis that the property investor agrees to take on the mortgage payments and other outgoings on the property therefore allowing the "seller" the opportunity to move on.

The clue of their operation is in the name in that the buyer "leases" the property from the seller and has an "option" to purchase it at some stage in the future.

The idea is that the investor has an option to purchase the property for a pre agreed figure by a future date and until that time they sublet the property for a figure in excess of the mortgage that they are paying. On that basis they could get a positive monthly cash flow and the prospect of a capital lump sum in the event that they exercise their option to buy and can sell the property at a profit.

Sounds great in theory in that the investor could assume responsibility for a number of mortgages and have a few thousand pounds a month coming in without ever owning the property and taking any risk.

Indeed I am told there are a good number of people who have made a great living by doing just that.

The risks however can be enormous for both parties. For the "seller" they are still responsible for the mortgage as far as the mortgage company are concerned and therefore if the investor does not pay the mortgage then the mortgage company will issue proceedings against the original borrower even though they no longer have control of their home. In addition by granting a lease arrangement to the investor the "seller" should have consent of their lender which is unlikely to be forthcoming on the basis that the lenders security is potentially compromised. As a result many presumably do not notify their lender and when the lender finds out they may consider calling in the loan in its entirety.

The seller is lured on the basis that the investor will exercise their option and purchase the property but they are under no legal obligation to do so. In short if the property is worth more than the option price then the investor will sell the property to exercise his option but if the value remains the same or falls then the investor will simply walk away and leave the seller with the same or worse financial issues than they had at the start. An option is exactly that – it gives the option holder the ability to either buy or not buy.

The other obvious problem for the seller is that because they will still retain their home and their mortgage, if they are wanting to move on they are normally restricted to rented accommodation rather than being able to purchase again.

From the investors point of view they may see that they will procure an income in excess of the mortgage payment but they run the risk that the mortgage rate will increase as a result of the risk perceived by the lender or alternatively rates in general may increase. That being the case the investor could have a negative cash flow from an investment, which could potentially have no value. The only advantage to the "buyer" in such circumstances is that they can possibly simply walk away from the situation.

Whilst I am an investor, as are my Clients, I have a moral aversion to this kind of deal, which is potentially bad news for the seller. My view remains that there are plenty of deals to be done which genuinely benefit both sides of the transaction. I would struggle with my conscious to know that I was procuring a profit to the potential acute detriment of the other party.

Consider the following example. A couple were trying to sell their home, as they desperately needed a bigger house due to a growing family. They were in negative equity to the tune of £25,000 having bought their current home at the height of the 2007 boom. They owed £125,000 on their house but its current value was around £100,000. Unable to sell in the traditional way for a sum that would cover their mortgage they elected to sign a lease option deal whereby an investor would take on the mortgage and take an option to purchase the property in three years time for £125,000. Delighted with this plan they went and rented a bigger property nearby.

The investor installed tenants in the property and failed to make the mortgage payments. The property is being repossessed and the sellers are responsible for the £25,000 shortfall on the mortgage. So now they have no house, an additional £25,000 debt and their credit rating is decimated. Hardly the new start they were looking for. From the investors point of view they have had a few months rent from their tenant and left a trail of devastation in their wake. Reputationally for the investor, not ideal.

There are currently, to the best of my knowledge, no real pieces of legislation in play in this area of investment and perhaps if there were more structured guidelines I could be more receptive to the model.

Investors in Scotland should be particularly aware that my understanding is that Lease Options have been outlawed in Scotland since 2011 not least given that there is no compulsion for the investor to purchase the property and therefore the seller can be left in the lurch.

EDC's:
Theoretically a slightly fairer system is the EDC or Exchanged and delayed completion arrangement. The way this works is that the seller physically exchanges contracts with the purchaser so they have sold the property but completion is delayed for a period of time, normally 3 – 5 years.

The advantage here against a lease option is that the seller has sold the property. The investor has bought the property and will, from exchange of contracts, maintain the mortgage payments and other outgoings until the sale completes. During this time the investor will let the property and derive an income from it in the event that the rent exceeds the mortgage payments and any other outgoings.

For the investor this can represent a good deal. In the event that the market is rising the investor can put together a portfolio of investment properties without initially putting in very much money. The risk to the investor is similar to that of the lease option but with the added pressure that in the event that the property prices fall over the period he still has to complete the purchase and financing that in such circumstances could prove a real challenge.

The risk for the seller is similar to the lease option with the exception that the purchaser is obliged to complete the purchase rather than merely having an option to purchase. One caveat I would add is that many of the investors undertaking EDCs are using a SPV (Special Purchase Vehicle - effectively a shell company with no asset) to undertake the contract. The risk is that in the event that they decide not to complete the purchase they will simply close the company down and leave the seller high and dry. This may be my cynical mind in overdrive but I have been involved in property investment for too long for it not to have crossed my mind!

My view for Clients is to be careful with these types of arrangements. If you want to be a property investor then my preference would be to purchase property in the traditional way and do a deal which works for all parties. Neither the Lease Option nor the EDC are regulated and both rely to too great a degree on the performance of the other party. This is, in my opinion, what makes them risky and unsatisfactory for all but the most risk hungry and aggressive of investors.

There is however an alternative of property investment which has soared in popularity over the last couple of years. It works on the basis that the property is not sold at all. It works on the basis that you let a property from a landlord and then you sublet it for more money, the difference being your profit. It is essentially a sub let.

Sublet:

This type of arrangement has been commonplace in the commercial property market for a number of years but of late it has become commonplace in the residential market.

This is a very established concept but one which has recently received an enormous amount of attention in the property industry. I am not aiming to compete with the reams of books and webinars that are available on this topic but I suppose a book on property investment should at least make mention of it.

In broad terms it can work in one of two ways. In the first instance the investor undertakes to let a property *for* a landlord at a set rental. This is on the understanding that the investor can then sublet the property to a number of people and collect a rent greater than the one they have agreed to pay. The difference is therefore the investor's income.

The advantage for the landlord is that he is then removed from the headache of tenants having only the investor to deal with and he saves a management fee from a letting agent, as the investor will manage the property as part of their function.

The typical type of property that people look for when considering a sublet is a three plus bedroom property perhaps with a second reception room so there is scope to rent out say four or five rooms on an individual basis.

If you are to take my locality as an example then a 4 bedroom Victorian house would let to a family at £800 a month. If it were let on a rooms basis then you would be looking at 5 (4 bedrooms plus dining room) sets of £300 per month giving the investor a profit of £700 every month.

Investors should be aware that this scenario effectively means that the Investor is acting as an agent on behalf of the landlord. On this basis they should be registered with one of the property redress schemes in order to comply with the new legislation which appeared in October 2014.

The second way of undertaking a sublet is where the investor lets the property *from* the landlord in that he or she becomes their tenant. They then sublet as described above.

A number of self proclaimed experts in this field have been running seminars to detail how investors can earn £5,000 or £10,000 a month without ever owning a property.

In theory this could work but it is not without risk. Furthermore there is an ethical issue in that the investor is cramming as many people in the property as is possible and has no incentive, given that he does not own the property, to improve or maintain the premises save but what is required to ensure its ongoing rental income. The net result could be the creation of ever declining accommodation, which at one stage will fail to achieve the income required to cover the rent that he himself is paying to the landlord.

Many investors that undertake such schemes use a licence agreement for the tenants rather than an assured shorthold tenancy. Whilst this book is not designed to provide the complete legal system surrounding property it is prudent to mention that in some circumstances these agreements could be construed as shorthold tenancy agreements.

Furthermore there is a suggestion that the agreement could indeed be a commercial tenancy and that the sub tenants may have a statutory entitlement to a new tenancy in the same way that the 1954 Landlord and Tenant Act works to protect commercial tenants such as shopkeepers. In an extreme case the landlord could in fact lose control of his property.

A more obvious issue with the subletting of rooms is that the property could be deemed to be a House in Multiple Occupation and therefore in need of a licence together with upgrades to fire protection and the like. Most houses designed for a single household occupation will not have such measures and someone is going to have to bear the costs of upgrading the property.

This is aside from the fact that the sublet agreement may fall foul of the landlords mortgage conditions and requirements of their building insurance.

Whilst I appreciate that potentially the scheme could work, there are so many potential pitfalls, my personal view that it is not for me.

The obvious issue with this proposal is that you do not control the property that you let. You do not own it nor do you deal with the issues of ownership.

Some people I have met undertake this strategy as their sole strategy whilst others use it as one strategy in conjunction with their strategy of buying investment property.

There are advantages and disadvantages to both arrangements but it is not my intention to go into any further detail within this book.

So there are some methods where you could get involved with property without needing to secure a mortgage or actually purchase the property before you derive an income from it. If none of these are for you then you can still start work in the world of property without having the funds to buy a property yourself. For example you could look at Deal Sourcing for other investors or Land Identification for Corporate customers. You could even simply sell leads of motivated sellers to property investors, or participate in an equity purchase scheme. I shall briefly consider these in the following paragraphs.

Deal Sourcing:
Regardless of how much money you have you cannot buy every property that comes to the market and therefore it may be the case that you could source property for other people. Indeed many investors specialise in different types of property and therefore you may source a property which is unsuited for your own requirements but which may suit another investor. You could therefore charge them a finder's fee and allow them to acquire the property.

Many firms retain surveying practices for just this role and all I am suggesting is that you could undertake it for other individuals.

I have a client who is particularly fond of commercial property which may have possibilities for residential redevelopment. I have another Client who wants land in Kent where he can build small schemes of 3 – 10 houses and I have another client who only buys ex-local authority houses.

By understanding the investors needs you can find property for them and once you have amassed sufficient finder's fees, then you can purchase a property for yourself. The process of acting for others in dealing with agents, understanding values, looking at the local planning system will never be wasted as ultimately you are going to be investing in the same area!

The costs of setting yourself up as a deal sourcer could be very low. To give you an example, I attended a landlord meeting recently where an investor saw two terrace houses being offered for sale on someone's feed on Facebook. He contacted one of his investors and managed to sell them to him and made a £10,000 profit without leaving his chair. It's a fairly extreme example but it does demonstrate what is possible.

Land Identification:
This is more a regional job for somebody. It basically involves identifying a number of companies who are looking for sites and then trying to present to them a site for which they will pay you an introductory commission. There is a lot of legwork involved here and your car will certainly rack up the miles but the rewards can be superb. It is not unusual for a fee of £25,000 - £30,000 to be paid to an introducer who finds a site for a company. Generally the acquiring firm will provide a remit in terms of the towns they are looking at, the size of plot they require, any road frontage requirements and what types of existing buildings they will consider. Just flicking through one of the trade press magazines I found a firm looking for sites suitable for petrol stations, a company wanting land for a high density student development and a well know fast food chain looking for sites for Drive-Thru restaurants – With a combined commission opportunity of £100,000 that should be enough to get you started!

In the past I have introduced sites to, amongst others, Majestic Wine Warehouse, Pizza Express, McDonalds as well as some of the regional and national housebuilders.

Most of the firms looking for sites and premises actually advertise their requirements in some of the property trade journals and so if this is something that you wish to get into then I suggest you head to the library and grab a copy of the Estates Gazette or other trade journals.

Lead Generation and Sale:
There are a few property people out there who simply generate leads of motivated sellers and sell them onto property investors. The leads can be procured through websites, google adwords campaigns and other sources. The purchaser buys the leads and then works through them in the hope to find people within that list who are keen to sell a property at a keen price. The challenge here is to encourage people to purchase leads without really knowing the quality of them. Whilst I can see the merit in doing something like this I would like to be a little closer to the action!

Equity Sale:
More recently I have seen schemes where a property seller will sell the beneficial interest in their property namely that they will sell an investor part of the equity that they have in a property. It is an interesting concept but again one which, in its current format, I remain uncomfortable with. If the seller has a mortgage then that mortgage company will have first charge over the property. Additionally for the investor to realise their investment the property will need to be sold, unless an investor can be found to purchase the equity interest, which will mean additional costs of estate agents and legal fees all of which will

eat into the investors portion of the money. Furthermore in the event of mortgage difficulties the lender could appoint a receiver or repossess the property and either the costs of the receiver could destroy your equity stake or the sale price following repossession could mean your equity interest has no value.

My concern with such arrangements is that they are likely to be offered by those people who are unable to raise funds in a traditional way or who are in financial difficulty. Imagine if you invested in the £10,000 equity in a property but unbeknown to you the seller was £2,000 in arrears with their mortgage, the property is then sold and once the arrears, estate agents and solicitors fee are deducted and the mortgage redeemed you are left with very little. A final note of caution is that there is, to the best of my knowledge, no real trading arena for these types of investments and so they may be difficult to sell in the event that you wanted to get your money out.

An alternative is to perhaps consider the shares of firms that invest in property. There are several out there and they operate in a more regulated way meaning that they are more easily tradable.

But hopefully your plan will be to purchase an investment property (or maybe several) in the more traditional way. If so, then before you do so there are a few things we need to be clear on…

CHAPTER 3
THINGS TO CONSIDER BEFORE YOU BEGIN.

Continuous effort, not strength or intelligence is the key to unlocking our potential. Winston Churchill

A recurring question I am asked when I do presentations is *"What characteristics are required to be a landlord?"* There are good landlords and there are bad landlords. As with any profession the most effective people are those who genuinely have an interest and passion in what they do. This is also true for property investors.

As well as absorbing the contents of this book you will need a genuine interest in property in order to succeed. Whilst this is rather obvious it is still worthy of mention. In any walk of life the most successful people are generally the ones that are most passionate about what they do.

I recently spoke at an entrepreneurship forum at my former school, Eltham College in South London and there were five former pupils presenting, all of who had set up very different businesses as diverse as a business providing marketing to sports brands, an events company, a recruitment company and a business recovery specialist. The common thread amongst all of them in terms of the key to their success, was that they were passionate about what they were doing.

Additionally as a Buy to Let investor, you need a genuine interest in your tenants and a passion to ensure that the property in which they live is appropriate for their needs and meets the legislative requirements.

One way to do this is to consider the tenant as your employer. You have to keep them happy or they won't pay you. If you upset your employer then you won't have your job for too long - the same is true with your tenants. If you keep them happy they are more likely to look after the place, more likely to pay their rent and more likely to stay in the property for longer. There is absolutely no upside to treating tenants poorly as you, the landlord, can be the only loser.

I caveat the above with a note to confirm that there are some people you simply cannot work with. Those who moan incessantly about the property, those who will not ever pay the rent on time or those who cause issues with neighbours and the like. If you find yourself in this situation then possibly the best thing is to bring the tenancy to an end. Just like a job there are some positions that just don't work out. Rather than remain miserable - do something about it.

Another characteristic the investor should have is to also appreciate that this is an active rather than a passive investment. Sure, it is likely to outperform the return from a savings account or an investment in stocks and shares or even your pension plans but unlike these passive investments, property requires some input from the investor in terms of time and resources. If you are unprepared to expend this effort then you are unlikely to enjoy your property investing nor are you likely to be able to maximise the opportunities it could give you.

Another thing that the property investor should bear in mind is that there is a continual requirement for learning. Aside from the existing legislation which impacts landlords there is a continually evolving legislative framework which a landlord must adhere to. You will have heard the phrase that ignorance is no defence and never is this more true than in the context of landlord and tenant.

Initially I read around the subject to educate myself and clearly then had the practical experience by acting on behalf of Clients. My view is it is important to have a good working knowledge of the legislation that impacts the landlord and tenant environment. Not only will it make you a better landlord but it will probably fuel your enthusiasm for what you are doing even further. If you are going to operate in this area then why would you not want to try and become an expert in your chosen field?

So those are the general characteristics as I see them.

Let's assume that you are ticking all the boxes and still determined to succeed as a property investor.

Whilst, as I have described in the last chapter, there are a number of different property investment types that you can look at I am going to assume that we are decided upon a standard Buy to Let investment.

Before heading down to your Estate Agent to see what they have, you should think carefully about what it is you are wanting to achieve from your property investment.

Growth or Income

Depending on your own investment goals you will, relatively early on, need to ask yourself the question whether you wish to invest for income or growth. Whilst the most common answer to this question is *"We want both!"* it is fair to say that generally speaking some properties offer better growth prospects whilst others offer greater income opportunities. Rarely do they offer both in the same measure.

Those who are wanting property to replace a pension will generally be looking for an income. Those who want property to allow them to leave their normal day job will also probably look for income and those who are trying to use property to get them the funds for a new venture, to buy bigger family house, to support or expand their business etc. will probably look for growth.

In broad terms an investor will look for income and the challenge for growth is more usually the preserve of the property developer.

There is no right or wrong answer here. It is just a case of deciding early on what your goals and aspirations are and then electing a strategy which will mean you can achieve them. Many investors do get to achieve both but it is important that you appreciate which means more to you, as it will impact what you buy and where you buy it.

To put this into perspective if I was looking for capital growth then I would be looking to buy in an area which is likely to receive significant inward investment. One example may have been to buy in Stratford ahead of the Olympic village being built or to locate in Ashford in Kent ahead of the international station and Channel Tunnel being operational. One current thought in my area is that following the closure of Manston Airport there is talk of the site being redeveloped as an enormous business park. More than one individual has since mentioned to me that they are now looking to buy in Thanet. Acquiring in such areas early on may mean the scope for rental income is less available but you are buying on the basis that there will be an upswing in prices. Many investors, particularly from overseas, have acquired property in London with the hope of capital growth. The income for them is secondary.

For those whose game plan is income they are likely to look at a more established residential marketplace where tenant demand is established and ongoing. Examples could include buying property in University towns with the aim of renting to students or areas where there is a high dependency on welfare with the plan to rent property to those in receipt of housing benefit. Alternatively you may wish to focus on areas which have a couple of major employers and therefore plenty of professional people looking for accommodation. Indeed I used to act for a Client who purchased property all over the Country provided it was within half a mile of a hospital. Her view was that staff are always looking for accommodation and due to the often anti social hours that they work, they are keen to live as close to their work as is possible.

Another interesting question is who makes more money, the investor or the developer? Over the longer term the investor can do really well provided they do not have to sell during a downward cycle however developers do not have the work of dealing with tenants and property management issues. As one person once said, *"Do not wait to buy real estate, buy real estate and wait"* suggesting that the investor could yield the better return. I suppose the answer is that both can make a really good living. Indeed some property people I know actually do both. One of my Clients who I would also regard as a friend owns around 100 residential properties which are let to tenants and additionally he, with his developer hat on, builds around 10 new homes a year.

So equipped with your financial aim for your investment you now need to decide how you are going to finance it.

Leverage and gearing.

Some would be landlords are in the lucky position of not requiring a mortgage and can buy a property outright. Whilst this is an enviable position for some people, thought should be given as to whether this is the most sensible option available to them.

In order to illustrate this point let us assume that the investor is considering purchasing a 2 bedroom terrace house in an area where such properties sell at around £100,000.

Buying the property for cash the figures would look like this:

Rent on property	say £575 pcm
Mortgage Payment	£0
Gross Profit	£575 pcm
Net profit after say 22% tax	£448.50 pcm

Value on day 1	£100,000
Value after 1 year	say £102,900

Alternatively if the landlord was to use borrowed funds then his £100,000 could purchase two properties and the sums could look like this.

Rent on property	say £1150 pcm
Mortgage Payment (50% at 5%)	£416.66
Gross profit	£733.34
Net profit after 22% tax mortgage allowable	£572.08
Value on Day 1	£200,000
Value after a year	£205,800

By buying cash you would have a total gain of say £8282 per year but yet if you took a mortgage and purchased two properties then you would have a total gain in a year of say £12665 i.e. 53% more!

Using this very simple example you can see that using finance in property investment can be a very prudent thing to do. Not only does it allow you to build a portfolio more swiftly but also given that the amount of the mortgage is fixed then the value of the mortgage debt will get eroded over time by inflation. UK inflation has never run at negative figures and indeed house prices have, over time, generally outperformed inflation. The use of mortgage debt is therefore a superb way to profit from inflation. Indeed in real terms the value of the mortgage could decrease by 50% over the term of the mortgage just as a result of the effects of inflation.

One other advantage of using borrowed money for a Buy to Let is that the monthly cost of the mortgage (the interest portion) can be offset against tax. In this way you have a tax efficient method of using inflation to reduce the amount in real terms that you owe.

Another example of using mortgage finance is that some mortgage products have additional incentives such as cash back or free legal or survey fees, which you would otherwise incur in the event that you purchased the property for cash.

A final thought is with regards to the opportunity cost of your money. If you use your own money to purchase the property then you would forego any interest or return that you would otherwise get if it was on deposit or invested elsewhere.

As a sobering thought I had a client a couple of years ago to whom I suggested that they could perhaps consider some borrowed funds for a property purchase. The alternative was that they were going to cash in their premium bonds for the purchase. They decided against a cash buy and purchased with a mortgage, leaving the premium bonds intact. You have probably guessed the rest of the story but to put you out of your misery about six months after purchasing the property they won £5000 on their premium bonds. I know this because the day they banked the cheque they bought me possibly the biggest box of chocolates as a thank you for my fine suggestion!

It is also the case that in the event that a mortgage is secured against a property you are far less likely to be a victim of identity fraud. Fraudsters tend to look for let property that is unencumbered of a mortgage. Not that this is a reason to finance a purchase when you otherwise don't need or want to, I just think it is an interesting point to make.

Mortgages for buy to let purchases can be a useful way to accelerate the development of your portfolio or to allow you to purchase earlier than would have been the case if you were buying for cash. Whilst you will no doubt have heard the phrase "Don't run before you can walk" there is an argument to accelerating a property portfolio if the market is moving upwards quickly or is expected to do so in the short term. Effectively you can book your purchases at todays prices rather than potentially having to pay more in 6 or 12 months time.

Whilst the foregoing broadly remains the position I do appreciate that the mortgage market has fundamentally changed over the last few years. To give you an idea of how much has changed I shall take you back to what I call the boom years of 2003 to 2007.

During this period I had a number of clients who were building significant portfolios of Buy to Let property with very little of their own money.

At the time, there were several strategies that they were adopting. Amongst the most popular was that the investor would raise a 25% deposit by undertaking a further advance on their main residential property. This meant they had the deposit for their buy to let property at a competitive residential mortgage rate.

They would then raise a Buy to Let mortgage for 75% of the value of the property that they were looking to buy meaning that their Buy to Let property was effectively bought with 100% borrowed money.

For those who had an appetite for more than one property they would then try and remortgage the buy to let property given the house price growth and enormity of appetite from the mortgage lenders to take out some money which would form the 25% deposit on their next buy to let property which they would similarly mortgage at 75% meaning that property was also bought with 100% borrowed monies.

At the time at least one of the mortgage lenders was offering to allow a remortgage almost immediately the property was bought. This meant that for some investors they could extract any money they had put into the property and even take some additional money out of the deal almost the day they bought the property.

This strategy worked for many for a period of time as prices were increasing and mortgage lenders were keen to lend. The difficulty came after 2008 when the lenders retrenched from the Buy to Let marketplace and prices in some areas fell by 30%. For someone who has bought a property with 100% borrowed money a 30% drop in prices (or indeed any price drop at all) will plunge them into negative equity.

I had a number of clients who had used this method to purchase 50+ properties inside two to three years. Some have managed to hold on to their portfolios during the recession whilst others have sadly not been able to.

The current position with regards to mortgage lending for the investor is a far more prudent one as far as the banks and other lending institutions are concerned. For example, most lenders now require the applicant to have a permanent job and a salary in excess of £25,000 whilst many want a rent coverage amount of 130% if interest rates rose to 5%. Interest only loans are less available than they were meaning that the differential between mortgage payment and rental income is far smaller than was previously the case.

Notwithstanding there are now an increasing number of Buy to Let products coming to the market place and so many would be investors will still, I am sure, be able to secure a mortgage.

For those who do not have the required deposit there are still a number of options available to you. Perhaps you could consider buying jointly with a friend or family member? Whilst you would then only get half the income and half the capital growth you would also only have to pay for half of any expenditure associated with the property. Not only that but you may, particularly in the early years of your property career, appreciate the support and camaraderie of working with someone else.

More recently there have been more novel financial offerings coming to the market. I am no expert on any of them but we now live in a world where crowd funding, peer to peer lending, Venture Capital and Angel Investor monies all play their part. I suppose what I am saying here is that if you fall outside the traditional Buy to Let mortgage criteria there is still no need to give up on your dream of becoming a property investor.

What if you have tried every avenue for finance without success and yet you still want a career in property? Well you could revisit Chapter 2 where there are some suggestions of how you could pass the time whilst still being immersed in property.

Let us for the moment assume that you are able to secure a mortgage for your proposed purchase. Before you leap for joy, just make sure you are in agreement with all the terms and conditions of that loan.

I offer this advice as I myself have recently suffered on one of my own Buy to Let loans. I took a mortgage out with a Building Society some years ago and it was a tracker rate which mirrored the Bank of England Base rate. I had been enjoying heavily reduced payments given the base rate has been 0.5% for 5 years. What I hadn't bargained on was that buried in the small print of an accompanying booklet to my mortgage was a clause which the lender suggests allows them to increase the rate if they so chose to do so. The lender did indeed increase the rate for my loan and I understand, for 6000 other mortgage customers and so as at time of writing my mortgage is around double the amount I would have expected to pay with the base rate being at 0.5%.

Whilst there is some consumer legislation in place you should bear in mind that greater protection is offered with residential mortgages than Buy to Let ones.

Those acquiring property with Buy to Let funding should also pay attention to the level of Loan to Value and establish whether, in a falling market, you would be obliged to make payment to the lender to rectify any loan to value breaches. Just be very careful in terms of your borrowing as recent experience has shown banks can move swiftly from having a huge appetite to lend to having a similarly large appetite to get the money back in.

The other point worthy of mention here is that you should ensure that your chosen solicitor or conveyancer is approved by your lender. Historically it was unusual to find a firm that was not approved but this has changed significantly now and it is currently commonplace that lenders will not agree to use sole practitioners. Whilst you are still entitled to have such an individual act for you, you would then need a different solicitor to act for the lender and this will doubtless result in a bigger legal bill for you.

Repayment or Interest Only:

A further question you should consider before taking the plunge of property investment is, assuming you are going to take a mortgage, whether that loan is an interest only or repayment loan.

The difference is very straightforward. With an interest only mortgage you pay only the interest on the loan for the duration of the loan and then repay the amount borrowed in full at the end of the loan. The alternative is a repayment situation where each month the payments are higher but at the end of the loan term there is no lump sum to pay off.

It would be prudent to take professional advice from an accountant, financial adviser or similar to determine the best for you but in broad terms if you are planning on selling the property at some time in the future and you are investing for income, then it is possible that an interest only loan could suit. It will allow a greater income during the period of the loan and allow a greater benefit of inflation working in your favour against the mortgage debt.

That said the availability of interest only loans has been seriously reduced over the last few years and many lenders are only offering competitive rates on loans which are granted on a repayment basis.

For those investors that wish to leave an unencumbered property or portfolio of property to their children for example, then often a repayment loan will tick more of your boxes.

In making your decision please remember that in offsetting the mortgage payment against tax you are only able to offset the interest portion of the loan and therefore not all of your payments under the term. Sorry to burst the bubble of those of you who thought they had just identified a wonderful tax loophole!

There is an argument for economies of scale and there is a strong argument for using gearing and leverage but I am increasingly seeing a reluctance to rely too heavily on Bank finance. There are a number of reasons why this may be the case. I hear stories of big investors who are under huge pressures from their banks due to perceived loan to value breaches, stress testing, onerous revaluations and the re-pricing of their loan products. This is often despite them never having missed a payment. It seems the reason for this could be purely as a result of a change in direction of the bank from wanting to increase its loan book to now wanting it all paid back. I have clients who have lost portfolios, clients who have been made bankrupt and clients who have been subjected to margin calls and several more who have had and continue to have, many a sleepless night.

Set against this backdrop it is easy to understand the investor who has changed their own model and would rather now have 10 properties with no mortgages than 100 properties all with a mortgage. Indeed I think moving forward there will be far fewer landlords with 100 or more properties in 10 years time than is currently the case. Having said that I see no reason why the number of landlords with a handful of properties will not increase over the same period.

My personal view is that some banks have, in some instances, behaved appallingly and should be brought to task. Consequently for my personal portfolio I would not want to gear myself more than 50% so that, in the event that the bank or economic climate become difficult, I can take comfort in the knowledge I could probably take my custom elsewhere. With a portfolio geared at 75% or 85% in static or falling market, your options for refinancing are almost nil.

So we now know our investment strategy and how we are to fund it. We are getting closer to letting ourselves loose on the Estate Agent but before doing so we should have a think in terms of what we want to buy and indeed where we want to invest.

When I was an Estate Agent the *"Should we go for a flat or a house?"* was quite often the first question that the potential buyer would ask. The answer depends on your aims and aspirations and what you are hoping to achieve. Let us consider both options in turn.

Apartments:
Flats/Apartments are very commonly purchased by buy to let investors as they are in the main cheaper than houses and are generally popular with the profile of people who are often looking to rent, namely those first away from home, young couples just starting out and pensioners trading down and looking to rent in their retirement.

I own some flats and they do very well for me but you must bear in mind that they have a finite life as far as a tenant is concerned. For example young couples have a tendency to start a family and once this happens their needs change and they often look for a house with some outside space or a property with an additional bedroom and the like. Young professionals often leave flats after a year or 18 months as they go on to buy a property of their own.

For those of you who have decided that income is your driver, a flat may be a more prudent investment, as the yield, even allowing for a modest ground rent and service charge, will probably be higher than with a house.

Another point to bear in mind is that it is increasingly the case that people have pets and a number of flat leases prohibit pets. This may mean that you are looking at a smaller potential pool of tenants. For those with a Rex (or in my case a Bruce) or a Tiddles (or in my case a Scabby) they may not be able to take your flat.

Houses:
Houses generally offer a slightly lower gross yield than apartments but that said you do not have the liability of ground rent and service charges in the same way you do with a flat. In addition tenants tend to stay longer and it is not unusual for tenants in my houses to stay 5 + years in the same house.

Depending on the area in which you invest, you will probably find that there are generally fewer houses available to rent. On that basis your house is likely to be in greater demand and therefore let more quickly.

Whilst it may not be true of all areas, my personal experience is that I have found that values of houses withstand economic turbulence far better than apartments. I remember when I was a first time buyer back in the mid 1990's, I managed to find a two bedroom house within my budget but the prices of the flats had completely collapsed given that first time buyers did not need to buy a flat as a stepping stone, they could go straight to a house. For that reason in 1995 we had flats on our books for sale at less than £25,000! I accept that nowadays these apartments would probably be attractive to buy to let investors however I can confirm that the price of flats in my area absolutely collapsed during the most recent recession from around 2008 not least as Buy to Let funding dried up at the same time.

On that basis, those of you looking for capital growth may be better with houses as opposed to apartments. There are no hard and fast rules but it is something that you should certainly think about.

Part of the conundrum of whether to invest in a flat or a house will invariably revolve around the question of leasehold or freehold.

The property investor needs to be aware of the principal differences between freehold and leasehold as leases have the potential to impact value and impact the investor's income ability.

Freehold pretty much means that not only do you own the property but you own the land that it sits on too. Leasehold in contrast means that you have the right to occupy a property and the land on which it is situated for a term of years beyond which the freeholder (the person who granted the lease) gets it back.

Some people think that just because a lease has say 70 or 80 years on it that it is little different to freehold. This is not the case. Whilst this book is not designed to be a legal textbook on Land law it is probably important to give you at least some basics.

The lease of a property reduces over time and whilst, once you have owned the lease for at least 2 years, you can insist the freeholder extends it, they are allowed to charge for the lease extension. In addition to the costs of the lease extension it is normal that you pay the freeholders legal costs associated with doing so.

The cost of the lease extension is a calculation, which looks at three distinct things including the reversionary value, injurious affection and marriage value. Without getting technical, once a lease has 80 years or less the freeholder is allowed to charge for marriage value and therefore the cost of the lease extension can significantly increase. Inexperienced investors are probably best advised to avoid leases with less than 80 years unexpired and indeed many mortgage lenders are uncomfortable when asked to advance funds on flats with shorter leases. Consequently, you should not underestimate the costs of a lease extension when deciding to purchase a leasehold property. I have just been asked for a lease extension on a property in my area for which one of my companies owns the freehold. The lease is down to 56 years, the flat is worth £137,500 and the cost of lease extension has been calculated at between £18,000 and £20,000. These are not insignificant sums.

In addition to an ever declining lease, the leasehold property will generally also have a ground rent and service charge payment which are payable. The Ground rent is fairly self-explanatory. It is a rental that you pay to the freeholder for occupying the land, for the duration of the lease. The payment is annual, payable in one or two payments. The service charge is the leaseholders contribution to the freeholder for things such as building insurance, maintenance of a Lift, Gardening, window cleaning, cleaning of communal areas and such like.

Investors should always refer to the lease prior to purchasing a leasehold property. The ground rent need not be a fixed figure indeed it is probably more common to find a ground rent which perhaps starts at £100 a year and rises throughout the term of the lease often doubling every 25 years. The lease will also detail the things that the freeholder can charge for as part of the service charge. General ones are building insurance, management, maintenance of the exterior and communal parts of the building. Landlords should pay attention to the detail. You do not for example wish to be contributing to the maintenance of a lift if you are buying a ground floor flat nor indeed would you want to contribute to the cleaning, electricity and redecoration of the common parts if your flat has its own front door at the other side of the building and you have no access to the communal parts. Sounds simple but I am staggered by the number of people who either, do not understand the lease or have not even read it.

The service charge element is also worthy of consideration when considering a purchase. Arrears of service charge can carry with the sale of the property so whilst the property may have been advertised at a really cheap price, if you factor in the outstanding or impending service charge demands, you may wish that you had never purchased at all.

In my experience, particularly troublesome leasehold properties are often placed in an auction. Whilst the auction house would have you believe that this is because this is where the specialist buyers go, my view is that they are put in an auction catalogue in the hope that a zealous buyer puts up their hand to bid without first taking a thorough look at the legal pack. Never has the term 'caveat emptor' been more appropriate than in an auction room! Indeed it never fails to amaze me the number of people who do not read the legal pack before committing upwards of £100,000!

For these reasons alone many investors prefer to invest in a freehold house although bear in mind there are many investors out there who have made and continue to make, a superb living from renting out flats.

OTHER CONSIDERATIONS BEFORE BUYING

The next decision you need to make is to decide who you want to have as tenants. The reason I say this is that if you were looking for a property for your own occupation then there are some areas that you would not live in and some properties that just wouldn't meet your needs. The same is true of tenants.

To illustrate this point there is no point having a student property which is miles away from a University Campus nor a house share suited to hospital staff which is the wrong side of town for the hospital. Equally if you want professional working tenants in your properties you should do some due diligence to ensure that those jobs exist in reasonably plentiful supply in the area in which you are going to invest.

We then need to look at what sector of the market you are wanting to aim for. To take the two extremes you can either aim for the top end of the market and provide luxury accommodation in sought after locations or you may want to provide more basic accommodation at lower cost for those on low or no incomes. Alternatively you may want to focus your energy on the middle market of small to medium sized family homes. Indeed if you are planning to build a portfolio you may want a mix of all of these properties and tenant profiles to balance your return and balance your risk.

Depending on what you want will depend on what you can buy. There is little point buying an ex local authority apartment in a tower block and then trying to secure a corporate let for a FTSE 100 company executive. Similarly you will struggle to get the numbers to work in your favour if you buy a luxury penthouse apartment and rely only on the prevailing local housing allowance rate for the area!

Once you can identify your target tenant you can start to think whether the property you are considering would appeal to them. In my opinion it is no different to selecting a Birthday present. If you know the individual for whom you are buying very well then you are far more likely to buy them something they will really like. For this reason really try and think who your tenant is likely to be and try and get a good understanding of what it is they are likely to be looking for. If you can get this right then the property will let more quickly and you will endure fewer void periods.

My experience with my own residential portfolio has been in the lower to middle sector of the market. My properties are clean, tidy, safe and provide basic, affordable accommodation. There is better property out there but not better for the same rent. By going for this mass market I feel I have the greatest pool of potential tenants. My other rationale for this sector is that repairs in a luxury penthouse costing £2000 per month would most likely be far more expensive than in a £450 per month flat or £625 per month terrace house.

In formulating your decision of your market sector you should consider where you want to invest. Clearly looking to attract a high-end tenant in an area devoid of much employment or opportunity could be a greater challenge than you wish to take on.

Many landlords, including myself, look to invest in their own locality and there is nothing wrong with this. Others take the view that they will engage the services of a managing agent and so can invest anywhere in the Country. I have always invested in my local area. This is principally for two reasons. Firstly I like to be hands on with my properties, I like to oversee works, meet tenants, deal with issues and generally be involved and secondly I know the property market in my local area intimately. I know what has sold, what is for sale, I know the other dealers who operate in my area and I know the agents. This knowledge is incredibly valuable and it is something I don't have in sufficient quantity in areas outside of Kent.

So now you have decided on the investment aim, funding arrangement, type of property, the market place you want to operate in, tenant profile and the location in which you want to invest. We can now proceed to establish how you know which property will suit and what price you should pay.

So here goes....the part you have all been waiting for.....The Property Triangle.

CHAPTER 4
THE PROPERTY TRIANGLE.

It's easy to make a buck. It's a lot harder to make a difference.
Tom Brokaw

A search on the internet will reveal hundreds of properties available for sale. You need to know which ones could work for you as investments and to do that you need a simple but reliable model which will allow you to calculate the rent, the return you want, which us property people call the yield and the amount the property is worth to you as an investor.

The model I think you need is "The Property Triangle"

There is unquestionably a need for a structured model which allows property investment decisions to be made. Any Estate Agent will be able to tell you stories of people who have vastly overpaid for property or purchased property in areas where rental is all but impossible.

So we now know that poor investment decisions are made in property but before deciding on a model which can assist it is surely useful to understand why poor quality decision making is often evident in property. To follow are some of my suggestions based on my 20 years as an Estate Agent.

1: The system is designed against you.

The system in the UK is not designed to assist the purchaser at all. Estate Agents are almost exclusively retained by the seller to get the highest price they can for the property and so the purchaser is not able to use them for impartial advice. Very few purchasers use Buying Agents and so the seller is professionally represented by their Estate Agent and the buyer is not represented at all. It is an odd situation as many would surely be aghast at having to defend themselves in court on their own whilst the other side have the service of a top flight barrister. It is far from a level playing field. My Property Triangle will give you the answers that the selling agent may not wish you to have!

2: The purchaser is emotionally involved.
Generally speaking there are emotions at play when property is involved. People are drawn to property in terms of their personal tastes and preferences. These may have no impact on the value of the property or the amount of rent that it will attract. By factoring them in your offer you will in all likelihood overpay for the property you want or ignore the property that offers a better investment. If I had a pound for every time I have heard a buyer say *"the criteria for us buying a Buy to Let property is "Would we live in it ourselves?"* This is massively flawed, as the lifestyle, needs and requirements of the landlord are likely to be vastly different from the needs and wants of the tenant. By focussing on the likes of the landlord and ignoring the needs of the tenant it is almost impossible to purchase the right property in the right area from a property investment point of view. By the same token would you let your tenant choose a home for you and your family? Enough said!

3: Transactional data is historic and inaccurate.

Whilst house price data is freely available, it is generally at least three or four months historic, which means it is only useful in a static market. The UK so rarely has a static market that such data is, in my opinion, of limited use. Imagine using such data to base your decisions in 2008 where some areas experienced 30% declines in prices in a matter of a few months! I would even exercise caution using transactional data in a static market unless you can be confident that the price paid for the other homes in the street was competitive. Just because someone paid £150,000 for a similar property to the one you are considering, doesn't mean it is worth £150,000. The purchaser may have overpaid to be near his work or family or because they were desperate to secure a property following a divorce situation or because they did not want to lose the buyer on the home they were selling. In short you should not rely on other figures – you should calculate your own. That way you can be sure they are accurate. My Property triangle yields the correct results in both a rising, falling and static marketplace as the value is based upon the current achievable rental.

4: Property investment is often made in a geographical area where the purchaser has limited knowledge.
Many investors consider the purchase of property in areas where they don't know and in such circumstances it is incredibly important that they are able to make the right decisions about which properties to purchase. Many Estate Agents will see a "tourist" and perhaps offer them the type of stock that is likely to be less attractive to a local investor. By understanding the rules of the game for property investment you will know which properties to view and which to ignore. Having been an Agent myself I understand that the agent is retained by the seller to act for them. Whilst the purchaser is entitled to a good level of customer service, buyers should remember that the agent is remunerated on the basis that they

get the most money for the property and not by ensuring that you buy prudently.

5. Buyers generally have limited knowledge.
Generally speaking most people have little or no experience of purchasing property as an investment and are therefore prone to make some less than perfect decisions. More concerning is that people tend to use their experiences of purchasing a home for their own occupation as relevant experience when it comes to property investment. The two are very different. The phrase "a little knowledge is dangerous" is certainly true in these circumstances. Particularly, novice investors have no knowledge of Houses of Multiple Occupation, Selective Licensing, Article 4 and a host of other legislation which could and should impact their purchase decision.

6. Buyers are generally out of their comfort Zone.
Novice property investors are generally out of their comfort zone. This is not something that they do with any regularity. If you are a seasoned property investor then for a moment just consider something that is a major decision but one which is outside of your comfort zone. My example would be that I recently purchased a second hand van. I have very little experience in buying vehicles and no experience whatsoever in buying a commercial vehicle. My concerns were whether I had considered all the things that a prudent investor would have thought of and whether I was making the correct choice of vehicle and whether the price I was proposing to pay was reasonable. These are the thoughts that a novice property investor is concerned with and bear in mind the amount of money involved is far greater than was required to purchase my second hand Peugeot van! A model which provides the

investor with greater knowledge, greater confidence and therefore greater ability is clearly welcome. Knowledge and confidence on their own can pay dividends in negotiations.

7: Landlord has no experience of tenants, what they want, need and the market place that exists.

Often, property investors were last tenants either when they were at University or in their late teens. The market has changed enormously in the intervening years and a landlord needs to be able to understand the rental market in order to make an informed decision about which property to purchase. By ensuring that the property you select is suited to the needs and wants of your tenants you will minimise the void times and maximise the rental return that you will receive.

Additionally this book is trying to provide you with the knowledge and confidence that you can become successful at property investment. The main reason that you could go wrong is if you overpay for a property. Bear in mind every property has a value based on its location, rental demand and a myriad of other factors. To a degree it doesn't matter what you buy provided you don't overpay for it.

I met an investor some years ago who, prior to property investment, was a secondary school teacher. He had a keen interest in property but was not intimately familiar with the property stock, nor market trends in his area.

What he decided to do was to only buy property at auction. The reason he did this is that he thought that there was a limit to how far he could overpay for property given his lack of knowledge and so by being only one bid above the previous bidder he figured he couldn't overpay by more than about 5%.

It is an interesting thought process. I respected him for acknowledging his lack of property knowledge and his proactive way to protect his downside. This is not however a full proof method of protecting yourself as many auctioneers will be able to reel off examples of properties which have sold at auction for far more than they could have ever achieved as a private treaty sale.

I myself have bought and sold via the auction process. It is suitable for some property and in my personal opinion, not for others. It is however a very exciting way of buying property and a thoroughly enjoyable day out!

My teacher example above is, I believe, typical of many people who want to venture into property investment and this is why a model which calculates the offer price for you is surely worth its weight in gold or the price of this book as an absolute minimum!

THE PROPERTY TRIANGLE.

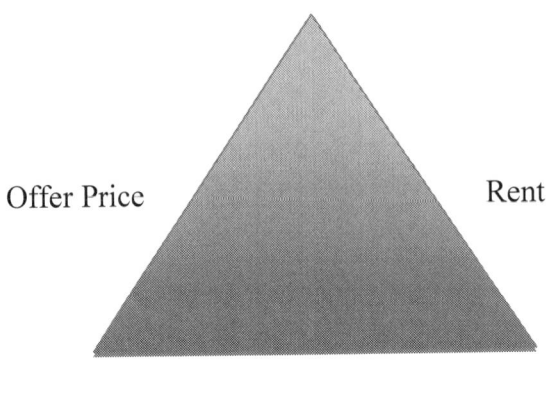

Offer Price   Rent

Yield

The Property Triangle

The Property Triangle is a simple investment model which will determine the price you should pay for a property, the rent that should be achieved and the investment yield that you will attain.

It is so called as it is reliant on three pieces of information in the same way a triangle has three sides and there is an interaction between each of the sides of the triangle.

With knowledge of the information required from two sides of the triangle you can calculate the information for the third.

I suppose in simple terms it is the property version of the Pythagoras' Theorem in that if you have information on two sides of a triangle you can calculate the details of the third. It is possible that Pythagoras could have adapted his Theorem for property calculations but at around 500 BC he was possibly a bit early for Buy to Let!

What is likely is that even if you failed to understand Pythagoras' Thoerem at school you will certainly understand and be able to use the Property Triangle! I say that with confidence as I was in the bottom Maths class for most of my schooling!

So if you know the yield that you are looking for and the rental value that you will achieve then you can calculate the amount you should pay for the property.

Alternatively, equipped with the price of the property and the yield you are looking to achieve you can assess the rental value you would need to achieve.

Finally, perhaps on a tenanted investment you would have the sale price and the current rental and you would be able to assess the yield the property produces and compare that with your expectations.

Before we get the calculators out it is important to understand the three components to the triangle:

Yield:
Yield is often described as the income produced by a financial investment, usually shown as a percentage of cost. For our purposes it shows the annual return that you will achieve set against the amount of money you have spent on your investment property. Most investors of single unit Buy to Let property in my area look for a yield around or just in excess of 6%.

For simplicity we are looking at the gross yield rather than a net yield which would take into account mortgage payments, service charges, repairs and the like. The reason being is that the aim of the model is to help you identify the suitability of an investment product not to calculate to the penny what you will earn from it in any given financial year. Notwithstanding if you wanted to calculate a net yield figure and then apply it to the Triangle then the calculations would work in exactly the same way.

Initially think of what yield or rate you want compared with the rate given by other investments. Banks are currently paying, in some circumstances, less than 1% for money held on deposit. Historically however rates of 3 – 4% were attainable. Property is a less liquid investment than a deposit account and so investors will tend to want a better rate of return. At this stage we are ignoring the return gained upon sale by any uplift in value and are concerning ourselves entirely with the rate of return generated by the rent. One consideration of a yield requirement is if you are going to take out a mortgage. If the mortgage rate is say 5% then I assume you are looking for a return greater than that.

One point to note is that generally the higher the yield, the higher the risk. Some small flats and property in poor quality areas can give a yield of 10% or more but the investment will almost certainly have higher voids, perhaps attract a lesser quality tenant and perhaps have more maintenance issues. Once these costs are included and a "net" yield is considered you may be better looking for something else.

There is no right or wrong answer but given the slightly illiquid nature of property as an investment you will no doubt seek a yield which will beat the return on a bank account, your mortgage rate and the level of inflation. Some people will accept a far lower yield if they are anticipating greater capital appreciation. This is a decision for you but let us assume for the moment you have selected that you want a yield of 6%.

Rent:
Unsurprisingly the rent is the amount that the property will produce in income over a twelve month period. Note that it may be necessary to apply a different figure to your calculations than that which is being paid at the property if it is felt that the current rent is not a market rent.

Examples of this could include where a tenant has been in residence a few years and the landlord has not increased the rent to mirror market conditions. In this case you may apply a higher rent. The opposite may occur in the event a tenant has been in a property since it was brand new or newly refurbished in which case they may, at that time, have paid a premium rent which would be unobtainable in the event you had to relet the property today. Be alert to situations where the rent is fixed, such as the tenant who is on a regulated tenancy or someone who has a long fixed term within an assured shorthold tenancy, even if the market rent is different. Bear in mind we are calculating our figures on what you can achieve.

Offer Price:
The offer price is the calculated figure that you would offer on the property bearing in mind the rent the property could achieve and the yield you want to achieve. By using this method you will be able to assess the figure you could go up to in such buying circumstances as tender or public auction. In a private treaty sale situation you will be able to assess the reasonableness or otherwise of a quoted asking price bearing in mind your investment yield requirements.

By understanding these three facets you can be sure that your property investment will work, be sure that the price you are paying is competitive and ensure that the income yield meets your expectations and needs – and all without having any other market knowledge. Now what does that do for your confidence as a Buy to Let investor?

Now let me talk you through each of the components so that you can understand how to make the calculations and start trying out the Property Triangle for yourself.

Yield:
This is going to be a fixed calculation based upon the yield that you are looking for. Provided you buy at the figure the property triangle suggests or less then you will ensure that your yield is the level you are looking for or better.

Assuming you want a 6% yield then the way we use this in the Triangle is by way of a decimal. So divide 100 / 6 = 16.67. Similarly if you wanted a yield of 7% then it would look like this 100 / 7 = 14.29. If you wanted 8.5% then you would calculate 100 / 8.5 = 11.76. I think you have got the hang of it now.

Rent:
The calculation that the Property Triangle will produce is only as accurate as the information that you start with and therefore it is important that your figures are as accurate as possible. For this part of the Triangle we need to calculate the annual rent that the property is capable of producing in the current market and in its current condition.

If the correct rent is £725 per month then we are looking at £725 x 12 = £8700.

One word of caution here. There is little point in using the rental value that the property will achieve once any refurbishments have taken place as in doing so you will end up calculating what you should offer on the property assuming those works have already been done.

If you have a situation where you are looking at a property where you simply cannot let it until comprehensive works are done then in those circumstances you can use the potential rental income calculation but remember to reduce the offer price the Triangle suggests you pay by the cost of undertaking those works. I shall show you an example of this later on.

If you look at the property portals rental section then you will find far more consistency in terms of pricing than if you look at the values at which property is offered for sale. Instead of the sale price for a 2 bedroom house varying, in my area, from say £85,000 to £150,000 you will see that the rental value of property in the area may vary from say £550 - £625 per month. This is incredibly important information as when used with the property triangle you will be able to calculate the value of the property as an appropriate investment.

Offer Price:
If this is the number you are trying to calculate then it represents the maximum figure that you should offer to pay for the property. If the property is advertised as "Offers in excess of", "Offers invited" or for sale at auction then you will be able to calculate your ceiling bid.

If you look on one of the internet property portals such as Rightmove or Zoopla let's say in an area with which you are unfamiliar you will find may properties which may look similar in terms of accommodation but at very different asking prices. One reason could be a variation in the expectation levels of the sellers or alternatively it is a reflection of the local market in that some streets are more popular than others. Being new to the area you are not going to know the difference and therefore you run the risk that you may buy a property in one of the least popular areas but yet manage to pay a price that could have bought you a property in a far more popular street.

Aside from being an incredibly helpful tool for Buyers and their advisers the Property Triangle is a very useful tool for Estate Agents in valuing property which is likely to appeal to property investors. Not only will it provide an accurate figure that is likely to result in a sale but it is also presented in a formula which is likely to make sense to the person selling the property. There were many occasions during my time as an Estate Agent where a vendor would strain to place a property on the market to reflect its owner occupation value as opposed to its value to the investor when the investor was the only likely buyer for the property.

To calculate the value to you as an investor you simply multiply the annualised rent by the decimal you created from your yield value. So a 6% yield and a £725 per month rent would look like this:

Annual rent £8700 x 6% yield decimal of 16.67 = £145,029.

So now you are competent in the three sides of the triangle let us look at the Triangle in action.

Firstly let us calculate a yield that a property is generating.

Example 1: Calculate the Yield
You are an investor looking for a 6% gross yield and you are offered a 2 bedroom terrace house for £99,950. Is it worth buying?

Firstly research the rent level as earlier described. Let us say the rent is £550 per month.

Annualise the rent ie. 12 x £550 =£6,600
Divide the annual rent by the purchase price ie £6,600 / £99,950 = 0.0660
Multiply the answer 0.0660 by 100 to give you a percentage ie 0.0660 x 100 = 6.60
The yield is therefore 6.6%

Let's look at this differently and assume that the estate agent calls you and says that they are inviting sealed bid on the property so you have no guide price to work with. How do you formulate your offer?

Example 2: Calculate the Offer Price

We have already calculated the annual rent at £6,600 and we know that we want a yield of 6%.
To calculate the price you should offer you need to create your yield as a decimal ie 100/6(yield required) = 16.67
Multiply the yield as a decimal by the annual rent ie 16.67 x £6600 = £110,022.
Therefore £110,022 is the maximum you should pay for the property in order to have a 6 percent yield.

For the third example we will calculate the remaining side of the Triangle namely the rent.

Example 3: Calculate the rent
For our final example we are assuming that you are offered a vacant property at £99,950 and you need to calculate the rent that you will need to achieve to maintain your 6% yield value.

Calculate 6% of the price of £99,950 ie. 99,950 x 0.06 = £5997.00
Divide this by the twelve months to give the required monthly rental ie £5997 / 12 = £499.75. In this case you would need to achieve at least £499.75 per month to return you 6%. Your investigations of rental prices as earlier described should mean that you have a strong idea as to whether this is achievable or not.

I mentioned earlier I would illustrate an example of a property which is currently unlettable unless certain refurbishment works are undertaken.

So let us pretend you are looking at a property in auction with a guide of £150,000 - £180,000 which needs £15,000 spent on it before you would achieve a rental. Once these works are completed you would, according to your research achieve a rental of £1000 per month. You now need to know whether you should bid and if so how much should you go up to?

Annualised Rent:	£1,000 x 12 = £12,000
Yield as a decimal:	100 / 6 = 16.67
	16.67 x £12,000 = £200,040

So an offer of £200,040 but there is an allowance of £15,000 for the essential works:

$$£200,040 - £15,000 = £185,040$$

In this case you could bid up to £185,000 and still maintain your yield requirement and so yes the property is worth bidding on!

To illustrate my earlier point of the importance of inputting accurate details let us suppose that you misjudged the cost of the essential works on this property and that they actually ended up costing £24,000 rather than £15,000. Let us assume also that the rental value is actually only £850 per month rather than the £1000 you initially thought. Look how that impacts the amount you should pay for the property:

Annualised rent:	£850 x 12 = £10,200
Yield as decimal	100/6 = 16.67
16.67 x £10,200	£170,034
	£170,034 minus essential works of £24,000 = £146,034

On this basis even the bottom end of the auctioneers guide price is too high and unless you are willing to compromise on your yield requirements you should not be bidding.

This is a sobering lesson. The same property and slightly different figures can make an enormous difference. Do make sure the figures you use are accurate to the best of your ability!

You must decide for yourself whether you wish to factor in any acquisition costs such as legal fees, mortgage arrangement fees and the like in formulating your offer price. This is purely down to the individual. Personally, I do not include them, my reasoning is that they apply regardless of which property I buy and therefore I base my calculations on the individual property rather than any generic costs. It is however up to you.

If necessary go over the above examples a few times with different properties that you have been looking at. For the doubters amongst you perhaps you could apply the Triangle to your existing properties or those of landlord friends of yours to assess its accuracy.

What you have just achieved is very valuable. With no market knowledge and no area knowledge and indeed no experience as a property investor and despite perhaps the protestations of an enthusiastic estate agent you have been able to determine whether a property is worth considering or not – Not a bad start!

Many novice landlords are nervous about purchasing investment property as they don't know whether they can gauge whether the price they are being asked to pay is fair. I hope you will agree that the Property Triangle provides you with the ability to bid with confidence on your next investment purchase.

There are a number of other methods of valuation that you should be aware of but my view is that my Property Triangle is the easiest for a novice investor to use. For completeness however I will consider a number of the methods used in the residential and investment marketplace by agents and surveyors.

Comparative Method of Valuation:
This is the one you would have been taught on a surveying degree when dealing with residential property and it is broadly the one which is used by the Bank and Building Society Surveyors when undertaking a mortgage valuation.

In simple terms you take the sale data of similar property in the area and make adjustments in terms of how the sold property compares to the one you are valuing.
The type of adjustment that you would make an allowance for could include exact location, decorative condition, size of garden, double-glazing, any extensions and the like. Sounds simple doesn't it! But what if you do not know your area really well? Well the allowance you make for the location or the period of time since the sale could be spectacularly wrong.

Not only is the method often used by building society and bank surveyors but it is also the principal method of valuation used by estate agents. It has its merits particularly when you are considering owner occupy property but it can really lose its way when you are considering the values of investment property. Let me explain why....

Imagine there is a new build block of flats being built and you want to purchase one as a Buy to Let investment. You are being quoted say £185,000 and the seller tells you that three apartments have sold at that figure.

What they may not tell you is that the three sales they have concluded have been to themselves in an attempt to set a valuation figure for anyone wanting to buy one of them.

I had a client who fell victim to this particular marketing tactic. He bought a property for £192,000 in a new build development, believing due to the above trick, that he was buying for 20% below the current market value.

Upon completion of the sale he walked into my estate agency office and explained that he had just bought this property and wanted to immediately sell it on and realize his profit. This we were happy to do. I asked him what he wanted it on the market for to which he replied it was worth £240,000. It wasn't. We had just sold others in the same block at between £130,000 and £150,000. Crestfallen we ended up taking it on to rent. Six years on it is still not worth what he paid for it and this is a lesson all property investors should heed when considering the comparative method of valuation.

Just as an aside, a similar trick can be played when developers detail the rent that a property may achieve. Imagine a new build developer markets their property to investors and offers a guaranteed rent of say £800 a month. The intention presumably is to convince the buyer and the banks surveyor that £800 is the going rate. It rarely is! The reality is that the property will get let at whatever the market will support and the developer will be liable to the difference for 12 months of the rent achievable and £800. It could be only a couple of thousand to the developer but will be less than if you had rejected the rent guarantee and instead haggled on the asking price!

You should also bear in mind the fact that there is normally a premium rent associated with a brand new property. I won't labour that point here as it is addressed elsewhere in this book.

To give you a further example, in my area, there is a road where a one bedroom flat will currently sell for around £50,000. At the end of that road is another road, which runs at a right angle to it where a one bedroom flat would be £100,000

- £120,000. So imagine that you do not know the area as well as me. You see the sale data of the flat at £100,000 and apply the residential comparative method and see nothing wrong in paying £60,000 for the flat in the next road. Your lack of knowledge has already booked you a paper loss of at least £10,000.

I regularly met surveyors during my time as an estate agent who acted for the Banks in undertaking mortgage valuations. On more than one occasion they made a comment which confirmed that it was more than a year since they had undertaken a valuation in my area. The comparative valuation method, in my opinion, only works when the Valuer has a good and up to date knowledge of the area in which they are valuing.

The Property Triangle is different as it looks at the value from a property investors mind. So using the last example with the triangle would work as follows:

Let's assume you want a yield of 8%. The £185,000 property would get a rent of £650 pcm so its worth to you is £97,500 and so at an asking price of £185,000 you would reject this one without even a viewing. Turning your attention to the cheaper flat and applying the same methodology (it would get £350 a month) would mean you would be offering up to £52,500. So regardless of market knowledge you should not overpay if you use my method of valuation.

Rebuild Costs:
There are some investors who work their property purchases on the basis that they like to purchase a property for less than it would cost to build it. This seems an odd way of looking at things but it does have some validity. It is however normally

only possible to find such a property in a depressed or recovering market place.

The way it works is that the investor will estimate a figure of how much it would cost to build say a two bedroom terrace house. Lets say they take the view that the cost of construction is £100 per square foot (or whatever the metric would be) and that such a property is in the region of 750 square feet. They would then arrive at a figure of £75,000.

On the basis that the property could be purchased for £75,000 or less then they will buy. Their view is that, at worst, they are simply acquiring free pieces of land. It is one strategy which goes some way to prevent you from over paying but it does not stop you buying in an unrentable area whereas the Property Triangle would!

Taking this method a step further I had a couple of clients who would pay the rebuild cost (or reinstatement value in property speak) plus 20%. They add 20% as they say that this is the opportunity cost of the planning, construction, period without income, funding costs etc. that would be incurred if they actually did have to build the property out.

The danger with this method is that it entirely ignores whether there is any rental demand for the property. If you were to purchase a property in an area where there is no rental demand then even if it is only £50,000, £75,000 or £100,000 you will have no real option to earn any money from it. By using the Property Triangle and incorporating the rental you would receive, the yield that you would want for that property, you may come up with a figure that is far less than cost of construction. Alternatively you may have just identified the perfect investment property.

Value Add method:
This is a pretty dangerous method to adopt for the novice investor as it normally means the buyer pays for what could be achieved rather than the price being reflective of the current position. Take for example a three storey house with the big garden in need of improvement. Its current value is say £100,000 but yet the seller wants £150,000.

The buyer is told that the house could be split laterally into three self contained flats and that a further smaller house built as two flats could be built in the garden. The resultant five units would be worth say £300,000 - £350,000 and the seller wants £150,000 to reflect 40 – 50% of realization value. Whilst this percentage of realization value can be a useful method for land with planning for multiple units it is rarely appropriate in the circumstances that I have used as an example. The asking price that the seller wants does not acknowledge that the purchaser will have to go to considerable effort and expense to try and secure planning permission (which he may not get), building regulations, will have no income during the build programme, will incur costs in funding the development and will take the risk of a market movement during the build programme. The canny investor should consider that if all these aspects are so easy then why does the seller not build the thing out and realize the additional value themselves?

If the above has left you a little confused then consider the following. Would you pay the same amount for Ford to deliver all the parts for their fiesta hatchback than you would if they built it for you? I thought not!

The other issue to watch for in this example is what is known as an uplift clause in the contract. These have become a little more popular with sellers in recent years. What it means is that whilst you have bought the property, the seller is entitled to a percentage of any uplift in value if you subsequently obtain planning permission or develop the site. In simple terms it can be described as a "having your cake and eating it!"

If you were to use the Property Triangle for your calculation of this example, assuming there is no uplift clause, then it would look something like this:

Income of property £650 per month, annualized is £7800. Looking for a yield of say 8% (triangle would suggest you pay £97,500) but will accept 7% on the basis that you accept that there is some future development potential of the site. Value given by the triangle £111,428. You may then apply a value to the potential building plot and the uplift in rental income from subdividing the main house. This would probably take you towards £150,000.

Alternatively if you were very confident in the ability to procure planning consents or if you were going to enter a conditional contract whereby you would not have to purchase unless the planning permission came through, then your sums may look like this:

Income of property £650 per month, annualized £7800.00
Projected income of developed scheme, 5 flats at say £500 per month each so £30,000
Assuming a required yield of 7% £30,000 x 14.29 would give you the sum of £428,700.

From this figure you would need to minus the costs of the development of say £100,000 for the new build of two flats and say £90,000 for the subdivision of the main dwelling leaving you with a bid price of £238,700.

You may want to reduce this further to allow for the build time through which you will derive no income.

Let us assume it's a 9 month build and so your loss of income is say 9 months at £2500. You would then make an offer in the region of £216,200.

The difference between the £150,000 and your £216,200 is the risk associated with obtaining planning and building out the development.

Income Achievable:
Whilst this method addresses some of the aspects of the triangle it is not foolproof. It does however provide a rudimentary basis of value particularly for commercial property. It works on the basis that you attach a value to the property at a multiple of the rent that is currently being paid. The multiple you add will depend on the property you are looking at and often the quality of the tenant but for a Buy to Let residential property you may wish to consider something around 7%, for a secondary commercial property with a less than perfect covenant you may want to see 10% or more.

As mentioned the method is not foolproof as you will, in the case of residential property, be unsure if the rent being charged is the market rent and in the example of commercial property the rent agreed may be historic a few years and therefore not achievable in the current climate.

Myself and a very good friend purchased a bar in a coastal town in Kent and secured a tenant on a 20 year FRI lease at £20,000 per annum. Since the start of the economic downturn, the number of pubs closing and the increase in people staying at home, the current rent achievable is probably nearer £12,000. Using the Income method at a return of say 10% you could value this property at say £200,000 yet its current value on the same basis is likely to be nearer £120,000. By researching the rent achievable and using my Property Triangle you will ensure that the £80,000 you would have just lost can stay in your pocket!

The triangle would look at the current rent achievable the required yield of say 10% and give you a value of £120,000. No chance of overpaying on this one!

When calculating values using the triangle you can make some adaptations when it comes to leasehold property. My suggestion is that you calculate the amount you would spend on building insurance and external decoration in the event that the property was freehold. Calculate the difference between what you would spend and what is charged and deduct that from the annual income that the property would generate. Then continue with the triangle calculation and you will arrive at the value you should be willing to pay for the property.

Let's take a look at an example: There is a two bedroom flat which would yield say £800 a month and you are looking for a 7% yield. The service charge is £900 per annum. You calculate that you could insure the property and redecorate the outside every 5 years for an annual cost of say £450. You calculate the annual rental at £9600 and you then minus £450 (the difference between service charge and what it would have cost you). Net income is therefore £9150, applying the yield you want of 7%

and using the Triangle calculations, you should offer to pay £130,714.

Whilst the triangle can make the correct calculations to allow for an extensive service charge you should be aware that a property with a high service charge may be a little more difficult to sell. On that basis you may wish to amend the yield you are looking for from say 7% to 8% in the event that you think the service charge is excessive. In which case you would want to pay £114,375 for this one.

Whilst I was an Agent, we were instructed in the sale of a two bedroom property where the lease was peculiarly constructed so that the ground rent varied in accordance with the value of the property. On this basis the ground rent was over £1000 and the service charge was coming in at a similar figure. We managed to get it sold but it achieved around 15% less than if the lease had been a little fairer to the leaseholder. Bear these things in mind when you are considering the yield you are wanting on leasehold property. Personally I normally look for an additional 1.75% on the yield for leasehold as opposed to freehold but it rather depends on what is realistic in the area where you have decided to invest.

One final word of caution with leasehold property is to always consider what the service charge may be in the future. Some freeholders have a reputation for high service charges and your solicitor may be able to give you some pointers in this regard. What you should look at is whether the property is in need of work. If the roof or something of similar cost is in need of replacement then there could be some heavy service charge bills on their way. Additionally you should consider how changes in legislation could impact the service charge. Recent examples include the need for blocks of flats to have an asbestos survey and fire risk assessments. As a result many very well maintained blocks have had huge service charge bills to cater for the removal of asbestos and the installation of fire precaution measures.

I have personally bought many leasehold properties and my aim here is not to frighten you. It is to make you aware of the considerations that should be at the fore when you are making an investment decision. Nothing is without risk but through understanding and management of risk your leasehold property investment can be successful.

Residual Valuation Method
Another method often used by investors although more commonly for investors who are considering reselling the property rather than retaining for long term rental, is the residual valuation method. This method is also commonly used when assessing the value of a site for development.

It is a method which will no doubt appeal to the organised amongst you as it involves a spreadsheet. Effectively you start with the figure at which you feel the finished development would sell for.

From that figure you deduct the costs and expenses associated with the property such as refurbishment costs, professional fees, interest on mortgage monies, council tax, utility bills, any required profit margin etc. etc.

The figure you are left with is the sum available to purchase the property. The difficulty with this model for the novice investor is twofold. Firstly, they are unlikely to know sufficiently accurately what the property would be worth once any works are undertaken and secondly, they are unlikely to know with sufficient degree of accuracy how much the works would cost and how long they are likely to take. For this model to work accurately the person would need to be a Valuer and Surveyor. In all other scenarios there is the potential for an enormous margin of error.

To put this into perspective I have formulated a residual valuation on the same property but with a margin of error on costings and the final valuation. Bear in mind this is the same property. You will agree this is a huge difference in valuations for the property in its current condition and you certainly would not want to be paying the higher one if the lower one is correct!

Works Required	Estimate of Costs

Exterior:

Rendering	0
Guttering and Downpipes	0
Roof	900
Scaffold	500
External Redecoration	0
Garden Clearance	0
Windows/Doors	0
Garden Landscaping	0
Building Work	0

Interior:

Communal decoration	0
Internal Decoration	1000
Kitchen	2000
Bathroom	1000
Plastering	0
Electrics	0
Heating/Gas	2000
Clearance	0
Boarding	0
Carpets/Flooring	1500
Damp treatment	0
Timber replacement	0
Plumbing	0

Fees:

Legal Costs In	900
Legal Costs Out	750
Lease Creation	0

Architects	0
Tenant evictions	0
Agents Buyers Fee	0
Marketing:	
Estate Agency Fee	1800
Staging	0
Holding Costs:	
Building Insurance	450
Council Tax	600
Mortgage Payments	0
Utility Costs	75
Wages	0
Total Costs	£13,475.00
Likely Sale Value	£135,000
Required Profit	£20,000
Works required	£13,475
Offer Price:	£101,525

This is an actual residual valuation which I undertook for a property I was considering although I must confess that my offer was rejected!

The astute amongst you will have noticed that I factored in my legal and other acquisition costs whereas earlier in this book I mentioned that I didn't do that. The reason they are in here is that this valuation is prepared for a property which I would have bought, refurbished and sold and therefore these figures need to be in there so I can accurately calculate an offer based on the profit I wish to generate. If I was planning on holding the property for rental then I would not include them but then again I wouldn't have used the residual method, I would have used the Triangle!

To illustrate the scope for error with a residual valuation let us re-run the figures and consider that you missed the following during your inspection of the property.

Some of the items in the back garden have asbestos and therefore you have to pay to have them removed £500.00

Some of the walls are lathe and plaster and will need reboarding and plastering. £1500.00

The electrical circuitry is in need of upgrading and so a new consumer unit and some upgrading is required. £600.00

You failed to spot that there is lead pipework in the property and therefore it all needs replumbing £1000.00

You discover woodworm in the roof void and some rising damp to the back wall. Roof needs spraying and the back wall needs hacking off, injecting and replastering £3500.00

These are all things that a novice investor could easily miss. Now look at how it affects the valuation.

Works Required	Estimate of Costs
Exterior:	
Rendering	0
Guttering and Downpipes	0
Roof	900
Scaffold	500
External Redecoration	0
Garden Clearance	500
Windows/Doors	0
Garden Landscaping	0
Building Work	0
Interior:	
Communal decoration	0
Internal Decoration	1000
Kitchen	2000
Bathroom	1000
Plastering	1500
Electrics	600
Heating/Gas	2000
Clearance	0
Boarding	0
Carpets/Flooring	1500
Damp treatment	3500
Timber replacement	0
Plumbing	1000
Fees:	
Legal Costs In	900
Legal Costs Out	750
Lease Creation	0

Architects	0
Tenant evictions	0
Agents Buyers Fee	0
Marketing:	
Estate Agency Fee	1800
Staging	0
Holding Costs:	
Building Insurance	450
Council Tax	600
Mortgage Payments	0
Utility Costs	75
Wages	0
Total Costs	£20,575.00
Likely Sale Value	£135,000
Required Profit	£20,000
Works Required	£20,575
Offer Price:	£94,425.

Assuming you had missed these things then you would have proceeded at the initial bid price of £101,525 and would have seen your target profit fall from £20,000 to £12,900. In fact it would probably drop even further as the increased works would mean increased time and therefore you would possibly owe another couple of months of insurance and council tax payments.

Just these oversights could reduce your profit by a third and if you missed something more major it could turn a potential profit into a terrible loss.

If this was being held for rental and you took out the fees and costs then the sums would look like this, assuming you used the Triangle for your calculation:

Projected Rent £650, Yield required 7.5%
£650 annualised £7,800
7.5% as a decimal 13.3
£7800 x 13.3 £103,740 minus works required that you did notice (excluding fees) £8,900
Offer Price: £94,840

So again for the novice investor the Property Triangle proves its worth as being more straightforward, possibly more accurate and with, in my opinion, less scope for error.

Thus far I have talked you through your investment goals, the tenant profile you are looking for, the area in which you are to invest and now I have equipped you with a newfound ability to value an investment property. The time has come for us to go out and find you one!

CHAPTER 5
HOW TO FIND A PROPERTY.

Try, Try, Try and keep on trying is the rule that must be followed to become an expert in anything.
W. Clement Stone.

As with so many other aspects of the property market, the search function has changed significantly over the years. When I started as an Estate Agent back in the mid 1990's, people used to telephone or visit our offices and ask to be placed on a mailing list. We in turn would take their details and post them out particulars of properties which we felt matched their requirements. Our busiest day for telephone calls was the day when the local newspaper came out with our full-page advert of properties for sale. Having said that, back then we had no email, no internet, no digital cameras and only one computer for each office!

Nowadays the vast majority of property searches are made online. I look on the Internet every single day for property coming onto the market in my area and yet I rarely peruse the property section of the local newspaper. Interestingly some of the estate agents now no longer undertake any form of print advertising and instead promote their properties exclusively online.

Most people have access to the Internet now either at home, work or even on their mobile 'phones. If you don't have Internet access and want a career in investment property then you are likely to become a very frequent visitor at your local library or Internet café!

There are a number of ways you can source property but probably the easiest place to start is one of the major property Internet portals such as Rightmove or Zoopla. Once you get a bit more familiar with searching it is useful to go on two or three of the major search engines as not all the estate agents upload their properties to all the web portals.

Before we move on to viewing and offering on the property you have found online, it is prudent to give some thought in terms of the Estate Agents you will be contacting following your online search.

There are lots of stereotypes about estate agents but what is key to bear in mind is that they are salespeople. Regardless of whether they are selling houses, dusters, cars or photocopiers they are there to sell and the more they sell then the more they earn.

For that reason it is imperative that you do not waste their time as if you do they will see you as an irritant rather than a revenue opportunity.

The other thing to bear in mind with sales people is they generally do not like to be "wrong" and I will revisit this thought in a moment.

Please ignore the stereotype of an estate agent. You need to work with them, return their calls, do what you say you will do and perform when you say you will perform. If you let an agent down then you will never get a deal from them again. It's human nature. If an agent can make one call to a great quality buyer and secure his commission why would he not do that and instead ring all 400 people on his mailing list?

Having been an estate agent for 20 years I know that the stereotype is an unfair one. I have never used hair gel, never worn braces and never considered an offer for my Grandmother (although I do admit to driving a convertible Porsche!) Agents are professional people doing a professional job. Treat them well and you will find they will assist considerably in finding you the property you require.

Firstly though you need to bear in mind that in most market cycles there are more buyers than there is property to sell. On this basis the agent can almost choose with whom they deal and you need to be in a position where you are one of their chosen investors. For this to happen the agent needs to have confidence that you are serious, that you will buy and that when you agree to purchase something you will not pull out at the last minute and cost the agent their commission.

I am proud to say that I have never withdrawn from a proposed purchase and I have never renegotiated on price once a deal has been agreed. Furthermore I have always adhered to the timescale that was agreed. The reason I do this is that property investing is my job and I take my job seriously and I want others to take me seriously.

As someone once said *"your reputation takes a lifetime to build and just a moment to lose."*

Sometimes agents will take a property onto the market at, shall we say, an ambitious price. Now sometimes this overvaluation is as a result of the agent having an off day, the vendor being keen to try it at an inflated price or the agent suggesting an inflated price so that he or she is favoured with the Clients instructions as opposed to one of the other agents in the town.

Never suggest to an agent that they have overvalued a property as it is akin to accusing them of not being able to do their job properly. Instead I would ask whether the price was their Clients suggestion and whether they would consider something at a more commercial level. It delivers the same message but does not upset the agent. Remember if you upset the agent you won't be offered another property from them!

One caveat to this is the recent recession, during which time the market moved from being a sellers market to a buyers market. All of a sudden there were far more properties than there were buyers and I started getting calls from agents I hadn't heard from in a couple of years offering me property! To give you an example of how bad things got in my area I recall selling a fully refurbished 1 bedroom flat with direct sea views for less than £50,000. During 2010 I was able to buy flats in my area for less than £30,000. They have since risen to around £60,000.

Therefore I really urge you to put some effort into your dealings with estate agents. It may feel unnatural but I assure you it will pay you dividends in the long run.

Now a quick search on one of the Internet portals will show that there are hundreds of properties available through these agents and so how do you know which is the one that will suit your needs as a property investor?

To illustrate this point I have just conducted a search for Margate and there are 470 properties – How do I narrow that down?

Firstly have a think in terms of what type of property you are looking for. Do you want a flat or a house, how many bedrooms do you want or are there a specific set of roads that you are looking at?

Now think back to the last chapter where you became an expert in using the Property Triangle. You know what yield you are looking for and so you now need to research the rental levels that your property is likely to achieve.

Lets assume you are having a look in Margate. So the yield you are looking for is say 6% and you are wanting a two bedroom terrace house. Your research shows that they achieve around £625 per month in rent.

Using the triangle calculations you would come up with a bid price of:
100\6 = 16.67
Annualised rent of £625 = £7500.
£7500 x 16.67 = £125,025.

The way most of the Internet search engines work is that you need to select a location where you want the property and the price range. Most also give you an option of the minimum number of bedrooms. We know the area, the number of bedrooms required and now we know the price range.

Now we know what you can pay and where you want to buy, we can now get on and find the property.

Back on the internet you can set the location tab for Margate or wherever you wish and you state that you are looking for a 2 bedroom house and set the maximum price at say £130,000 - £135,000 to allow for some negotiation.

The search will return you a handful of results and amongst them is possibly your first investment property purchase! In my example we have reduced from 470 down to 9.

Now you are equipped to contact the agent and arrange some viewings.

Once you have located a property that appears to fit your criteria you should arrange to view it. It is absolutely imperative to view a property before you consider purchasing it. I have been involved in the purchase of over 150 properties over the years and I have never purchased a property without viewing it first. In my view to do so means you are taking a huge and unnecessary risk. When viewing you should try and look at the property through the eyes of someone who is likely to be looking for a property of this type and see if it would work. If the property is a two bedroom terrace then it is likely to generally appeal to a young family. There is therefore likely to be importance of some outside space for young children, a kitchen that can accommodate a table and two decent sized bedrooms. If there is only a small yard, the bathroom is downstairs and one of the bedrooms is a single then you may be looking at a higher void period and potentially a lower rent. If this is the case then you would need to recalculate what you should pay based on the lower rent projections.

If you are looking to let the property as an HMO then look at the size of the rooms, the number of bathrooms etc. I think you get the idea.

Whilst I do not expect you all to be surveyors there are a number of things that anyone can look out for when viewing a property. To follow is a little checklist that you may wish to bear in mind when you are viewing. It is important to be familiar with building defects because as well as offering leverage to negotiate a good purchase price, they will allow you to more accurately assess the suitability of a property in line with your plans.

External:
Guttering and downpipes.
Are there any obvious signs that they are broken or damaged? Is there any staining to the outside walls, which may suggest that, the gutters and downpipes are leaking or not working effectively? It may be they are simply blocked but it may be the case they need replacing and any damage made good.

Roof:
Are there any missing or slipped tiles? Are there any little metal pins which appear to hold the slates up? If there are more than 10 of these on a roof then the roof may need replacing. Is the ridge line (top) of the roof straight and level? If it is sagging it could suggest that the roof needs more support or the tiles are too heavy for the roof structure. Roof work tends to be expensive not least as it normally requires scaffolding. If you are able to have a look in the loft of a property take a look and see if you can see any water ingress or areas of daylight coming through.

Floors:
Are the floors solid or suspended timber. Have a little jump up and down while the estate agent is not looking and you should be able to tell. A suspended timber floor will offer some flex when you jump and a solid floor will not. If the floor is suspended timber then there should be air bricks allowing sub floor ventilation. Are they present, are they blocked? Without

sufficient ventilation the floor may be susceptible to rot or decay.

Walls and Ceilings:
You should have a close look at walls and ceilings. Are they likely to need replastering? Are the walls the old lathe and plaster or is it more modern plasterboard sheets? Are ceilings (and sometimes walls!) textured? Not only is this far from popular with occupiers, you should also consider that some textured coatings include asbestos. You should pay particular attention to the walls in ground floors and basements as they may be suffering from damp. Make sure you also look at the walls and ceilings upstairs as they may provide clues to roofing or guttering issues or indeed penetrating damp due to poor brickwork pointing.

Windows:
Are they double glazed? If they are double glazed, are any of the sealed units misted indicating they have failed and therefore need replacing? Open curtains and blinds and have a look. Its better to notice a defect before you have purchased the property! By opening windows you will also be able to tell if the hinges are working properly.

Electrics:
Find the consumer unit (fuse board to those of you over 40!) Has it got separate breakers that would trip out in the event of a fault? These are called residual circuit devices. Also, is there any green and yellow earth wire around the consumer unit and meter?

More recent installations will have the RCD devices and earth bonding to the meter and consumer unit. If you see old red and black cabling or cable covered in fabric rather than plastic then you should really budget for a rewire.

Gas:
Boilers really vary in terms of how long they last and so it is difficult to assess whether you are likely to need to budget for a new one. Back boilers (i.e. those which sit behind a gas fire) are normally a tell tail sign that the heating system needs replacing. Those with a balanced flue (which looks like a steel biscuit tin) are also worthy of closer investigation. Warm air heating tends to date from the 1970s and is a real "no no" for buyers and tenants alike. It basically blows dust round the house and is a real irritant for those with any sort of asthma of respiratory problems. If it has warm air heating then I would always suggest that you budget for a replacement system.

Wet Rot and Dry Rot:
Always be on the look out for rotten timber as it can be a sign that there could be more serious problems. Wet Rot is normally easier and less expensive to deal with than Dry Rot but repairs for either will eat into your budget.

Wet Rot is often evident in window frames and cills or around bargeboards and soffits. Where the damage is isolated to a certain area then it is normally possible to remove the affected wood and replace it.

Dry rot on the other hand is more aggressive and can spread considerably through a building and can, in serious cases, cause structural damage. It is often evident in skirting boards or timber flooring and for the alert amongst you it has rather a distinctive smell.

Whilst staring at floorboards and roof timbers you should also be on the lookout for woodworm. It is quite an easy one to spot as you will see small flight holes in the wood itself. The slightly trickier thing to determine is whether the infestation is current or old. To do this you should look to see if there is any dust around the holes suggesting recent munching of your timbers.

Damp:
Your nose could be your best survey tool for damp as you will often be able to smell it. Alternatively you could go on a viewing armed with a damp meter. Depending on the cause of the damp will depend on the cost of the remedy. It can be very minor or it could be incredibly serious and therefore very expensive.

Things to look out for are basements or areas where the floor level is lower than the ground level. In addition where the ground level breaches the damp proof course of the property or where there is damage to the render to a property or failed rainwater goods or failed pointing. If you see damp then think logically how it could be being caused and then you can start to assess what remedial action is required.

Structural movement:
The remit of this book is not to equip you to compete with a Building Surveyor but you should be alert to the tell-tale signs of structural movement. Have a look at each of the external walls of the property and see if they are straight or whether they bow or bulge. Lack of straightness could be as a result of poor quality construction but is more likely to signify movement. In addition you should be looking for serious cracks. Small cracks which follow the mortar joints of the brickwork are more likely to be settlement or thermal

movement but ones where the crack goes through the bricks themselves could be signs that the property is not very well.

Internally look to see if doors close properly or indeed whether they close on their own. Both could be signs of movement. If in doubt then get a surveyor to have a look for you. I have never done so but then again I have a surveying degree and have spent the last 20 years looking at property. If you have any concerns about the structure of a building then my advice would be to get them checked out by a professional. You will never be criticised for spending a few hundred pounds if it stops you wasting a few thousand!!

Asbestos:
Asbestos is no longer used in residential property in the UK but that has not always been the case. You should be alert to the presence of asbestos as, aside from the potential health risks, the cost of removal can be quite significant. Areas where asbestos were commonly used which you should look out for are on the back of airing cupboard doors, around pipework, in vinyl floor tiles, blown-in insulation and commonly in the construction of garages and outhouses.

The process of viewing and assessing the property is the same regardless of how you found the property in the first place.

So far I have just talked about looking at property on the Internet as part of your search efforts but there are other avenues you can pursue which may result in you finding the perfect investment property.

To follow are some other sources of property that you may wish to consider in addition to those offered by traditional estate agents

Auctions:

Purchasing property at auction is a very different method of acquiring property than the more traditional method of buying via an estate agent. For the experienced investor the auction house can be a good source of property with the benefit that as soon as the hammer falls, the property is yours. The advantages are that you can buy a property quickly, there is no chance of the sale falling through and you do not get involved in a lengthy chain.

Novice investors should be wary if considering purchasing at auction. Generally auction catalogues are released around three weeks before the sale and the legal documentation that goes with them is often only available a week or so before the auction. This leaves very little time for the inexperienced investor to view the property, establish what price they should bid to, peruse the legal documentation and arrange any necessary finance.

Investors should be aware that significant sums could be at stake in the event that your bid at auction is successful but yet you fail to complete the purchase 28 days thereafter. Non-completion can be for something as simple as the mortgage offer did not come through in time or because there is something wrong with the property or the legal documentation, which means that a lender is not prepared to lend. Both of these scenarios are a nightmare for the investor.

In the event that you are unable to complete then the seller is entitled to retain your 10% deposit. Furthermore if they then subsequently sell the property to someone else for less than you were paying for it then they can return to you and demand the difference.

97

My advice to investors on the subject of auctions is simple. If you are not 100% sure that you can complete the transaction in the time allowed under the term of the contract, then do not bid!

Whilst on the subject of auctions, I have had some success in the past in picking up property which was unsold at an auction. My view is that there is a psychological failure if a property does not sell at auction and therefore the seller may be deflated and really eager to sell. I have bought a few properties this way for a figure below the auction house original guide price.

If, on the other hand, the property is likely to attract lots of interest in the auction room then it may be worth your while approaching the auctioneer to see if the property can be acquired before the auction. The auction house normally have instructions to submit any pre auction offers to the client on the basis that they are in excess of the quoted guide price.

Bearing in mind my caveats above, let us assume that you are prepared to take the plunge and bid at auction. Initially you will need to register with the auction house and provide them with your name and address and the details of the solicitor who will deal with the conveyancing should your bid be successful. In return you will be issued with a bidders number, which you will hold aloft in the auction room in the event that the bid is the winning one.

To the best of my knowledge there is no secret to how to best bid at an auction. Some people will tell you that you should never be the maiden bidder and that you should always wait for someone else to start the bidding. There is no evidence to suggest that this yields a greater chance of success. Others will tell you that the use of a "knockout" bid will get you the property you want. The way this works is, say that the bidding is going £50,000, £52,000, £54,000 then instead of £56,000 you would shout out say £65,000. The idea is that it will confuse and obfuscate the other bidders with the result being the hammer will fall before they get their thoughts together. Whilst I have seen this work in a couple of the London auctions I have also seen it used without any obvious advantageous result.

My personal view with auctions is that I do not bid until the very last minute. On that basis, if the property is going to sell for far more than I was prepared to pay then no one will ever know that I was interested in that property. If you are buying regularly and people know the sort of thing that you buy and what you are prepared to pay then that information can be used against you. In addition I sometimes bid over the telephone as there are a couple of investors who will buy something just because I am interested in it. One of them regaled the reason why as *"If you are interested in it then it must be a deal and it must still be a deal one bid higher than your highest."* Possibly true, so another word of advice is please refrain from describing to all your property chums the property you want to buy and how much you may want to pay for it. There is no upside to divulging this information! Besides, there will be plenty of time for that once you have completed and the property is yours!

The other word of caution I have is in terms of submitting a proxy bid. Such bids are submitted prior to the auction and work on the basis that you advise the maximum amount you will bid up to. The auctioneer will in turn bid up that figure. I have never bid in this way as I am nervous about such bids for the following reason – The auctioneer is paid by the seller of the property and acts in their best interest. They owe no liability to the buyer. If a property is guided at £100,000 and I submit a proxy bid a couple of days before the auction detailing to the auctioneer that I would like him to bid up to say £122,000 what is likely to happen?

To give you a clue about the answer, it is standard practice for auctioneers to contact their clients just before the auction. During this call they will detail to the Client the level of interest that has been shown in the pre auction marketing period and the number of legal packs that have been requested. This will give an idea on the number of people who may bid. Depending on the response the seller will have the opportunity to alter the reserve price of the property.

So in our example I want to buy the property for as near to £100,000 as I can but I am prepared, if absolutely necessary, to go to £122,000. Given that the auctioneer and the seller now know that I will go to that figure and that I have already submitted a 10% deposit for a purchase price of £122,000 what are my chances of getting the property for £100,000?

For those of you who are thinking that they could bid up their own property in an auction in order to achieve a higher price, whilst I understand your thought process, this is heavily frowned upon by the auctioneers and there is the added risk that if your bid is successful then you will have to pay the auctioneers fee and yet all you will have bought is the property you wanted to sell!

About a year ago, I was acting as a consultant for a Receiver who was placing a block of flats in an auction. They were guided at £450,000 - £475,000 but we were aware that we had one party who would be prepared to pay over £600,000. It was felt that no one else would and that the bidding would therefore not reach anything near to this figure. It was also not possible to change the reserve/guide price by such a significant amount so the decision was taken to remove it from the auction and to offer it at the following auction with a guide of £600,000. It was sold at the second auction for £635,000. If the bidder had kept his thoughts to himself then I believe at the first auction a figure in the region of £525,000 would have bought the block.

Again there is no upside in divulging your maximum bid prior to the auction unless you are negotiating a pre auction purchase.

A final auction trick you may want to consider as a property investor is to look at properties which are in auction houses far away from the property. My experience is that these can sometimes attract less interest and less bidding. There seems no reason why this should be the case nowadays with the availability of internet and telephone bidding but I have seen properties in auction houses 100 plus miles away from the property and I have seen them sometimes struggle to reach their guide prices.

Investors should be cautious at auctions. Such places are often the preferred method of selling property of non-standard construction, property where Japanese knotweed is the only developed garden plant and leasehold property with defective leases. Additionally however they are the place for unusual properties, ones for which it is difficult to assess a true value for or ones which are likely to receive significant interest or as has been the case recently place where the seller (often a bank, local authority or LPA receiver) has to demonstrate that the maximum price was achieved and the auction environment allows this. It is a myth that auction property is "cheap" as the following paragraph will graphically demonstrate.

There is a chap who lives near me called Paul Ribbons. I have never met him but his reputation precedes him. He makes a living from the auctions rooms and what he does is fascinating. He buys a property on the open market and then, as he puts it "distresses" it. This may be partially removing a kitchen or boarding up windows and the like and then he places it in auction with a very competitive guide price. His plan is that the investors will see that it hasn't been owned long, it is guided at less than was paid for it six weeks earlier and therefore the seller must be desperate to sell. With a plethora of investors thinking the same, the interest and bidding could be high and he will actually turn a profit on the thing. There must be some truth in it – he has evidently made a really good living out of doing just that!

Having been an agent as well as being an investor I have seen many properties sell at auction at a price higher than I believe could have been achieved on the open market. I have also seen many properties attract very few bids and sell at a level which I think is markedly less than could be perhaps achieved on the open market.

I must admit I still find property auctions exciting even though I have long since lost count of the number I have attended. If you are considering bidding at auction then it may be a good idea to attend your local auction to get a feel for how it works and the various bidding methods that people adopt.

Buying from private ads:
There are occasionally private adverts for property which appear in the local newsagent windows, local paper or on the

Internet. I have never bought in this way but I would be receptive to doing so. Provided you make a thorough inspection of the property and have your legal adviser check all the paperwork there is no reason why the purchase could not go smoothly.

One alternative, which a couple of guys I know do, is to have leaflets delivered to houses in areas where they want to buy and offering the owner a quick sale without the need for an estate agency fee. It may yield some results and I suppose if you got one good deal as a result then it would pay for the costs of your leaflets many times over.

Personal Contacts:
The final consideration for property sourcing is through your existing contacts. Let people know you are investing in property and you may be surprised with what you are offered.

Just a couple of weeks ago my partner Vyckie was out walking our dog Bruce and a fellow dog walker said she had inherited a house in our area and wondered whether we would be interested in buying it. Two hours later and I was stood in her lounge making an offer for it. The more networking you do the more people you talk to the more property you will get offered.

Many people groan at the prospect of networking. It is not a new thing but in the property world it is fairly unavoidable. The good thing is that effective networking will really pay you dividends.

The reason why networking is so essential is that there is a very finite availability of property that will meet the requirements of a property investor.

To give you an example let us assume that the average branch of an estate agent will bring to the market 10 – 15 properties per month. Out of that 15 they will, if you are lucky have 1 which fits the criteria of the savvy property investor. If you then consider that the average branch office of an estate agency may have 400 + people registered with them looking for a property, how are you to ensure that you get the call when this gem comes to the market?

The answer is by networking! You need to build relationships with agents and others to ensure that you can get a chance at the stock that you are looking for.

Indeed you should even try and make friends with people you meet at auctions and on sales viewings. Many investors offer opportunities to other investors and this in itself can be a good source of stock. For this reason you will find that people will try and network with you once you start your journey in property investment.

It's actually quite fun. If I am booked to go to an open house then, depending on the property type and price range, I can almost predict the people who will be there. Get to know the other investors that operate in your area. They can be a help rather than a hindrance. Also if you get to understand the type of property they are after then you may be able to find a niche type of property with far less competition that you could focus on and indeed the other investors may actually start referring such property to you.

The same is true for local solicitors who may be dealing with probate instructions. To be successful at property investing takes more than "right place, right time." It takes networking, building and working relations. If you are looking for a solicitor to befriend for the purpose of probate instructions then my advice is to find a very long established firm with deep roots in your locality. They are most likely to have the most extensive probate division. Alternatively if you are unsure which to pick then have look on their websites and find the one who has the most staff dealing with probate and Estates.

Many investors I know place adverts in shop windows and in the free papers and even on websites such as Gumtree. Whilst I accept that this may yield the odd result I am convinced that the way to get the right stock at the right price is to work with a selection of estate agents in the area in which you wish to invest. I have done this myself and have often been given the opportunity to view and purchase property which is "due to come to the market" and as such has not been seen by anyone else.

I have also been given the opportunity to purchase property for less than a seller has been offered elsewhere as I have the reputation that I will never pull out of a purchase and that I will generally get the matter exchanged within 14 days and completed within 28.

CHAPTER 6
SECURING A PROPERTY.

Patience and perseverance have a magical effect before which difficulties disappear and obstacles vanish.
John Quincy Adams

So you have sourced a property that you think is "the one." Perseverance is now the key to get your offer accepted and move through the process until the purchase completes and you can collect your keys.

Making your Offer.
If you are buying by private treaty, the offer stage is often one of the most exciting parts of property acquisition and I hope that by providing you with a few pointers, you can negotiate your way to a great deal on your investment property purchase.

The first thing to bear in mind when dealing with an estate agent is that they are acting for the seller and they are employed and financially incentivised to achieve as much for the property as they possibly can.

You must bear this in mind at all times as it can be easily forgotten if the agent is being nice to you, you appear to have struck up a good relationship with them or he/she has offered you a coffee. Never forget, the more you pay the more the agent makes.

With this at the fore of your mind you should submit an offer and have the agent believe that the offer represents the maximum you will pay for the property. Not sure why? Then look at the following scenario.

A property investor has been looking at a property for £130,000 and asks the agent to submit an *initial* offer of £120,000. The flaw here is that they say the offer is an initial one and thereby implying that they will make another. The agent contacts the seller and says that they are pleased to report that they have received an offer of £120,000 for the property. The seller asks the agent what their thoughts on the offer are. The agent is likely to say *"Whilst it is a decent initial offer may I suggest that we go back to the prospective purchaser and see what they will go up to."*

Surprise, surprise the offer of £120,000 is rejected.

Now consider the following:

The prospective purchaser says to the agent *"I have seen a number of properties in the area and I am in a good position to proceed and therefore looking for a deal. The absolute maximum I would pay for that property is £120,000, could you have a chat with the owner and see what their thoughts are?"* The agent then phones the owner and says they are pleased to report they have an offer of £120,000 . The owner then asks the agent for their thoughts on the offer. The agent replies *"well I appreciate that you may have been looking for more for the property but the buyer is unwilling to go any higher and it is worth bearing in mind they are in a position to proceed with the purchase quickly."*

If you were the seller, under which circumstances would you be more likely to accept that offer?

Another point to bear in mind is that you should try and second guess the sellers response or their next move. Using the example above where £120,000 is rejected the seller may say that they will reluctantly reduce to £127,500. The buyer may be minded to move to £122,500 and so the sellers likely response is that they may meet in the middle at £125,000. Try not to allow this to happen. In the event that the £120,000 is rejected then be bold in moving to say £122,000 with the absolute conviction that this is as high as you will go.

As an agent I used to really enjoy agreeing offers and getting the best I could for my Client. I recall those buyers who said something like *"Can you try them at £120,000 but let me know what they say as I wouldn't want to lose the property"* In such circumstances it is clear the buyer will pay more and so their initial offer will be rejected.

The more conviction you can add to your offer then the more likely it is to be seriously considered. In the past I have submitted an offer to an agent by email with the offer I am making, my solicitors details and proof of how the transaction will be funded. It shows I am serious and may mean that I can buy for a keener price.

I once had a Client who took this suggestion to the extreme. He used to make an offer and forward to the seller or their agent a sum equal to the 10% deposit with instructions to use the money as an exchange deposit or in the event that his offer was declined they should return the money. He managed to buy a block of flats for just over £1M using this method at a time when the block was attracting a lot of interest from other buyers.

One other thing you could try with your offer is submitting a more calculated looking figure. With the example I have used, instead of offering £122,000 following the rejection of your

£120,000 bid you may want to consider £121,980. The seller will immediately preoccupy themselves with how you got to that figure and you can confirm that based upon your calculations that is the absolute maximum you can pay. Not only will it give sound reasoning to your initial offer but it will force the seller to give the revised offer further consideration rather than simply discounting it and asking for more.

Another offer acceptance method I have used is the dual offer technique. It works on the basis that you offer them two figures based on two circumstances with one of the offers being the amount you know they will accept.

To put this in context let us say the property is being marketed at £130,000 and the agent has been back to you and said £125,000 is the minimum the seller will take. Using this method you would offer them £125,000 on the basis that the property is empty and that the seller undertakes a gas and electrical check and any remedial works and you will complete the transaction in say 2 months. Alternatively would they consider £122,000 on the basis that you will take the property with the current tenants and take on the chin any remedial works to the electrical and gas supply. As an added incentive at £122,000 you would aim to get the deal concluded in 28 days.

The offer gives you huge credibility in that you have offered what the seller wants but in all likelihood the time delay, hassle and various unknowns mean that they may well accept the £122,000 offer as their preference.

As an investor you are in a stronger position as the seller knows that you are not as emotionally attracted to their property as would be the case if you were planning on living there. In the right circumstances you could exploit this and pressure the seller into accepting your offer.

To illustrate this tactic you could say to the seller *"I have seen three properties, all of which would suit my needs and all of which would attract a similar rent. Rather than waste the agents time by offering on all of them, I would like to submit a maximum offer of £122,000 on your property. I would be grateful if you would advise me of your decision within 48 hours in order that I can either get my solicitor instructed or submit a similar offer on one of the other properties I have seen."*

The seller, instead of thinking whether you would pay more is now wondering whether they can snare you as a buyer in preference to any other sellers out there. Moreover the seller will be wondering whether the other properties are more flexible on price and whether they should just accept the offer and leave the other two vendors struggling to sell. It is a mindset change for a seller and it can really work.

As you become more confident it is all but guaranteed that your negotiating ability on offers will significantly improve.

Whilst I do not get every offer I make accepted, I have had a good degree of success in negotiating good offers – there is doubtless a skill to it and it is great fun!

Once you have got your offer accepted it is good practice to confirm the details in an email confirming also any other conditions of the offer. For example if you have agreed to pay say £120,000 subject to the property being vacant then make this clear in an email. It will save any issues later if the seller decides they do not want to evict the tenants before the sale.

Also make a note if you have agreed that the purchase is subject to a survey or anything else as you never want the agent to think you have moved the goalposts or are trying to change the terms of the deal as that could adversely affect your credibility as a buyer.

Once the offer is accepted you are on the road to your property investment. The first thing that will generally happen if you have agreed a purchase through an estate agent or auction house is that you are issued with what is known as a memorandum of sale.

This rather grandly titled document basically details the name and address of both the vendor and purchaser of the property together with their solicitors' details. Additionally it includes details of the property being sold, the price agreed, tenure and any special conditions such as a timescale to exchange contracts or in the case of an auction purchase, the date of completion.

The solicitor acting for the buyer will generally then receive a pack containing the contract and any supporting documentation from the vendors solicitor.

Within this pack is often the property information form and the fixtures and fittings list which will have been completed by the seller.

The property information form, as the name suggests, asks questions about the property, the answers to which the buyer may find useful.

The first section of the property information form concerns the boundaries to the property in terms of who owns which boundary, whether the seller is aware of them ever having moved and whether there have been any disputes. Another section asks whether there have been any alterations to the property and in the event that there have been, the seller is requested to provide copies of any planning permissions and the like. Section 5 details whether there are any guarantees with the property. These may include electrical warranties, damp proofing guarantees or a guarantee for a new roof. There is then a section on environmental issues such as flooding and more recently a section has been included asking the seller of there is any Japanese Knotweed at or near the property. The final sections of the form are concerned with the occupiers of the property and the various services that are connected to the property.

The aptly named fixtures and fittings form provides an inventory style account of the fittings that are included within the sale or which may be available at an additional cost. Virtually all sellers leave carpets and curtain poles nowadays but do have a thorough look through to ensure that anything you thought was included appears on the list as being included in sale. I recall a sale some years ago where the buyer negotiated directly with the seller and agreed that the AGA oven was included in the sale. It showed on the fixtures and fittings list as not being included but alas the buyer did not read it. I also recall a property I sold in Canterbury some years ago, where the seller said they would include carpets. On the day of completion the buyer discovered that the luxury wool twist carpets that were there when they viewed the property had been replaced with a far inferior carpet which could, at best, be described as fluffy cardboard.

Another document which often accompanies the property forms is the office copy entry from the land registry. It is essential you take a look at this one as appended to it will be a plan and you must ensure that the property you think you are buying and its plot is the same as what is shown on the land registry plan. As a point of interest the register of title document will normally show what the seller paid for the property if you hadn't already found that out!

The land registry documents may also include any restrictive covenants, rights of way or easements over the property. Your solicitor can advise you on these but you should make sure that everything on those documents works for you in terms of your plans for the property. Some covenants will detail that the plot can only ever house one dwelling and you would not want to have missed this if your plan was to build a pair of semi detached homes in the back garden. Others may state that the land can only be used for a private dwelling for one household. This may be crucial if your plan was to subdivide the building into flats.

At this stage the buyers solicitor will normally then apply for searches which are documents which notify whether there are any factors which impact the property or the immediate vicinity. The Local Authority Search, or Local Search as it is more commonly known, will highlight any planning or building regulation issues, enforcement action, road changes and parking restrictions which may affect the property.

It is an important document as it details anything which may impact the enjoyment or value of the property. Clearly this is important to you as the buyer but also important to whoever is granting you a mortgage!

The solicitor will also normally engage searches of the drainage and water authorities to establish whether water can be discharged to a public drain and the like.

Additionally many solicitors undertake Chancel searches to see if the property lies within a parish where occupiers could be charged for works to the parish. Whilst the risk is low, the value of claims can be very high and where a risk is established my view is that an insurance policy should be taken out to protect the owner of the property.

The background to chancel repair liability stems from land which was sold by Henry V111 in the sixteenth century. The theory is that current owners of this land are known as lay rectors and therefore funds can be recovered from them as a result of the 1932 Chancel Repairs Act.

Whilst many people I have spoken to seem to think that Chancel insurance is just a money making scheme for the insurance companies, my view is different. Upon my solicitors recommendations I have always taken the Chancel insurance. The well known Wallbank case illustrates the benefits of taking this cover.

The case concerned a couple, Mr and Mrs Wallbank who were given a farmhouse on former rectorial land. They were subsequently issued with a bill for around £100,000 for chancel repairs. The bill was challenged in court but unfortunately for the Wallbanks they lost the case and were left with a bill in the order of £300,000 once various legal costs were added

The law has changed from October 2013 but I would still suggest you speak to your solicitor and take advice on whether it is prudent to take out some insurance to cover yourself.

Don't panic if some of the documents don't make sense to you. A good solicitor or Conveyancer will be happy to talk you through them and they shouldn't let you proceed with the purchase unless they are satisfied they have the details that are required. Unlike the agent acting in the sale of the property, the solicitor is working in your best interest.

Once all of the information is gathered together and you and your solicitor are happy with it you will be asked to sign the contract. This is often a bit of an anti climax for a buyer as a typical contract is a two page prepopulated form rather than something more grand and important looking.

Signing the contract doesn't commit you to the purchase as it is the solicitors effective exchange of contracts which is where matters become binding on both parties. Despite the title 'exchange of contracts', the exchange is normally conducted over the telephone and indeed attended exchanges are reasonably rare nowadays.

The contract itself will detail the Buyer and the seller as well as the property address. It will also include the title number which identifies the property at the Land Registry. Importantly it will have the price agreed, the amount of the deposit and therefore the balance due upon completion. Any subsequent pages to the contract will detail any special conditions which your solicitor will be able to advise you upon.

Normally, if you are buying with a mortgage, the mortgage company will need five working days to get the monies to your solicitors account and therefore it is normal to exchange contracts with a completion date set for 7 or 14 days thereafter.

Many people believe the time to pop the champagne cork is on exchange of contracts as, at that time the seller must sell to you at that price and the buyer must buy, so theoretically the sale has gone beyond the point at which it can fall through.

My experience as an estate agent and as a property developer is somewhat different and I therefore reserve any celebratory activities until completion as the following tale illustrates.

Myself and a colleague purchased a redundant property in Margate some years ago with the plan to refurbish the property and to create seven sea facing apartments. Works got underway and we concluded a 12 month build which resulted in a stunning development with fountain, games area and some really funky exposed iron work. The whole front and side had retractable glazed panels so the occupiers could soak up the stunning sea views. Toward the end of the development we decided to market the property and selected a guide price just in excess of £1M.

We duly found a buyer who instructed their solicitors and eventually exchanged contracts paying a 5% deposit. Unfortunately they failed to complete, I presume as they were unable to raise the completion monies and whilst we were able to retain their deposit we also retained the building. That abortive sale was in agreed in 2007 and within a couple of months of the transaction falling apart, the market had dropped and the next best offer we received was £700,000.

We still own the property and I hope its value will continue to improve to the level it initially was but in the interim it is a constant reminder to celebrate only upon completion!

As an estate agent for 20 years, I was only ever involved with three transactions out of probably around 2,000 which exchanged but never completed. It is rare but it is possible!

CHAPTER 7
BOUGHT A PROPERTY – NOW WHAT?!

You must always be able to predict what's next and then have the flexibility to evolve.

Marc Benioff

So there you are brandishing the keys for your new property investment. You now have to decide what to do. There are a number of things that you may be thinking about such as letting, refurbishing then letting or selling, or simply doing nothing and putting the property straight back on the market to sell.

It is important that you have your end goal in mind when you start, as to decide further down the line will generally cost more money. To give you an example, if you were going to refurbish and sell a property you may be minded to install a kitchen complete with appliances. If the plan was to refurbish for letting then it may be prudent not to provide appliances and incur the ongoing repair liability that may come with them. Additionally the sale property for the owner occupier market may well have a better quality carpet than is required for letting. To get it wrong one way may mean the property is over specified for the letting market and therefore you have wasted some money. To get it wrong the other way may mean that buyers do not want to pay top money for your property as they feel the level of finish is lacking. Both situations can be avoided by making a decision at the outset and sticking to it.

The only caveat to this is if you are looking to sell the property to a Buy to Let investor. In such circumstances the specification for sale will be the same as for rental but unless your area is such that you are obliged to target a buy to let investor, you would be better pitching for an owner occupier as they will likely pay more for the property.

Initially, let us consider that your goal is to sell the property. To maximise your return you have a number of options to consider.

Adding Value:
The key thing to consider when evaluating the benefit of added value is to establish the ceiling price in your particular location. If your property is a three bedroom terrace property in a location of similar, then it is possible that a loft conversion could add value as could the creation of off street parking. Similarly Kitchen and Bathroom improvements could also be a wise choice. The addition of a swimming pool, summerhouse or sauna are however, unlikely to provide you with any return at all.

When considering adding value, try and imagine who would want to buy the house and what they would do to it if it were already theirs. Knocking through a small kitchen into an adjoining dining room to create a family room could, for example, really appeal to your target market.

You may have heard the term "ceiling price." This is generally considered to be the absolute maximum that a property will sell for given its location. Many developers, convinced that they produce a wonderful product, will aim to beat this ceiling price and in a rising market this is considered possible in the correct circumstances.

Of course there is a certain pride for a developer/investor to have sold the most expensive and therefore arguably the best property in a given street but this, in my view, should not be their goal.

The danger with aiming to beat a ceiling price in a road is that it relies on other people being comfortable in the price being a first for the road and that includes your buyer and their mortgage company.

Buyers are generally looking for the best deal they can get and unless there is a rapidly increasing market with little available stock, then buyers will tend to make offers against an asking price. It is not unusual for them to base their offer price on what similar properties in the area have sold for. Historically this was a rather well guarded secret unless the buyer wanted to make a manual application to the land registry for a print out of the office copy entry but nowadays this information is available on a myriad of Internet sites at the click of a mouse. All buyers will remember the recession and understand that values can rise as well as fall and it is therefore reasonable to think that they may be a little nervous of having the honour of paying a higher price than anyone else in the road.

Even if the buyer has fallen head over heels in love with your property, the buyers mortgage company is a more likely stumbling block. Their Valuer will tend to use the comparative method of valuation, which I have discussed earlier in this book and therefore base their valuation on the prices that have been achieved in the immediate locality. In protection of a later negligence claim against them by the lender, they are normally quite conservative in their approach and therefore getting them to agree to a new ceiling price can sometimes be an impossible challenge.

My view has always been that you should try and sell the property at a competitive price so the buyer thinks they have got a reasonably good deal. Whilst I may sacrifice the odd thousand or two on each sale I make, I am convinced the properties sell quicker and allow me to recoup my funds and move on to the next one. There is little profit to be made from a unit sitting on the market unsold!

So when considering adding value to the property I would consider what you could do to maximise the value of the property but yet remain within the existing price parameters of your street. Whilst digging out the basement and providing a Gymnasium and Games Room may be worthwhile in a central London property it will not yield you a positive return on a small Victorian terrace on the East Kent Coast!

Immediate Resale:
The alternative to the value add is to simply place the property back on the market and hope to make a profit. It may be that you have seen an angle which wasn't fully acknowledged when the property was initially marketed. A large garden may provide scope for a building plot, the property may offer scope for subdivision or you may simply have purchased at a price which allows an immediate profit upon resale.

If the immediate resale of the property is your goal then do be mindful of the costs associated with the purchase and sale of the property as they will come straight out of any profit margin you make. As a rough guide I always allow £2,000 for the legal fees of purchase and resale and 1.5% plus VAT as an estate agency fee. Add to that the costs of building insurance, any utility costs and council tax for the period that you own the property.

Let us assume it has all gone to plan and the property is looking its best or you are opting for an immediate resale without undertaking any refurbishment. It's now time to get it on the market and so another trip to the estate agents beckons!

In order to do this effectively you need a really good working relationship with the estate agent. When selecting an agent do not simply go for the agent who offers the cheapest fee.

Selling agents normally quote their fees as a percentage of the sale price. Not only to reduce the agents fee reduces their incentive to sell the property but the difference on a £150,000 property between 1.5% and 2% is £750. Is it really worth demotivating the agent by trying to haggle for a better commission deal?

Another option you have is to increase the motivation that the selling agent has to find you a buyer at the right price. This is something I have done in the past and it can work really well. In essence you agree a figure at which you are happy to sell the property for. You then say to the agent that on that figure they will get their 1.5% or 2% or whatever their commission rate is. You then say that anything above that figure you will give them say 30%.

The last time I did this I offered the agent 50%. I agreed that I would accept £100,000 for the property and pay their standard fee (1.5%.) I then said anything in excess of £100,000 I would split with them 50/50. Within 10 days we had a sale agreed at £106,000 with the agent set to receive £4500 as a fee and me ending up with £3,000 more than I had been happy to accept.

Many of you may be in shock at this revelation but it really is a "win win" situation. Not only do you incentivise the agent to sell the property as quickly as is possible but you give them a real incentive to achieve the absolute maximum that the buyer will pay, not merely the minimum that you as a seller will accept. Believe me it can work. Try it, you may be very pleasantly surprised at the results!

What you are looking for is an agent who you feel you can work with, who appears enthusiastic and determined to get your property sold and one which has a credible marketing reach. You may wish to also bear in mind in your selection process the agents who most typically have your sort of property on their books. This is for two reasons. If your selected agent regularly deals with the top end of the market and your flat is a budget 1 bed starter home then you may find that they do not attract the type of buyer you need. Additionally by aligning yourself with an agent that works within your market place should mean that they will give you a call when another suitable property comes available for sale. This is important as a trader cannot make any money without stock!

From my personal point of view the hardest part of property investment is trying to source the properties. From a sale point of view I have never taken more than a month to secure a buyer on any property I have elected to trade.

To successfully trade property you need to provide a property for which there is an obvious and ideally growing marketplace, present it to a standard that exceeds others available in that price range and offer it at a price which compares favourably to other properties the buyer may be looking at. Get all three right and it should sell very quickly indeed.

Given that the primary purpose of this book is to educate the budding property investor, I hope you have glazed over the last few paragraphs on the basis that you have decided to retain the property for rental purposes!

Assuming that retention is your goal, you have a number of options to now consider.

Immediate Rental:
It may be the case that the property is in reasonable order and that you can immediately rent it without having to undertake any improvement works. This can be a great solution as it means you will very shortly start to recoup some of the money that you spent buying the property.

Before you head out to the Letting Agent in search of your tenant, do consider whether if you were to do some works to the property, how that would impact the rent. In the right circumstances some works will add a disproportionately positive amount to the rent you achieve and therefore you could be earning 8% return not only on the property but also on the money you expended to improve it!

Certainly this is not true in all circumstances and therefore you should seek the professional opinion of an agent who knows your locality well and who has very up to date knowledge in terms of what tenants are looking for.

Adding Value:
Most professional property investors will do something to a property immediately they acquire it to ensure that it maximises its rental and in many cases, mirrors the standard of property that they have in the remainder of their portfolio.

Using myself as an example, I generally replace Kitchen and Bathroom fittings to each property I acquire, upgrade the electrical consumer unit and more often than not replace the boiler prior to the first letting. I always redecorate throughout and replace the carpets and vinyl.

Many investors find it very difficult to find properties which work when calculated through the Property Triangle, especially if they are looking for a relatively high yield. One option that you have is to buy at a level which the Property Triangle may not quite agree to and then add value.

In the correct circumstances this can increase the income and therefore the yield and bring an investment back into the triangle calculation.

Examples of such value adds can include the provision of a loft conversion. Done correctly this can mean the addition of an additional bedroom/bathroom and therefore considerably increase the rent achievable. Whilst you need to add the cost of conversion to the purchase price before calculating, using the triangle, it may make an investment more viable. The same can, in the right circumstances, be true in terms of converting an integral garage to create an additional bedroom or reception.

Side extensions to semi and end terrace houses can also be a good way to add value. Sometimes it is possible to add another house to the terrace and given that the property will cost only the cost of construction (the land has already been paid for) it is quite possible to create a brand new house which will work within triangle calculations. Again this would generally work for a Buy to sell strategy too.

More experienced investors will also look at adding value by the creation of planning permission or change of use. Currently there appears to be a trend of investors purchasing redundant public houses and then endeavouring to gain planning permission. A client of mine acquired a closed pub for £400,000 and then managed to get a planning consent for the conversion to 7 residential apartments. Once the conversion costs are added to the site purchase the resultant rent means that all 7 units will be triangle compliant which is a great deal in a market place where finding one property that fits the triangle is a challenge.

For the more novice property investor there are relatively cheap ways to add value. The replacement of Kitchens and Bathrooms with more modern fittings can increase the rental value of a property significantly. The provision of furniture to perhaps attract three students rather than a family can significantly enhance the rental value and indeed a basic redecoration and recarpeting can add anything up to 20% on the rent, in the right circumstances. In some areas just the creation of parking by adding a dropped kerb can make a significant difference to the rent that can be achieved.

Not all these methods will work in all areas and marketplaces. This is another reason why it is key to have a good letting agent on your side. They will be able to advise you in terms of what will add value and what will make no difference. You must ensure that every penny you spend has a positive return of some kind whether that be a likely reduction in voids, an increase in rental or an enhancement of capital value. If you ignore this and spend money on things that have no return at all then you will eventually run out of money – it is a simple rule of mathematics!

Buy and Refurbish:

This is a system which is tried and tested and can, in the right circumstances, work for you. It works on the basis that you purchase a property, undertake some improvement works and then rent the property at an enhanced figure than would have otherwise been the case.

This is a system I have and continue to use myself. By improving the property not only can you improve the rent that the property will obtain but also the quality of tenant that you will attract.

The other benefit is that you will be preserving the capital value of the property. A tired property is more likely to be purchased for a keen price than one which is ready to move into.

Consider the following real life example. A two bedroom house is on the market for £85,000 and would possibly rent in its current condition for £550pcm. This would give the investor a yield of 7.7%.

By spending £5,000 and improving the heating, retiling the bathroom, replacing the kitchen worktops, redecorating and recarpeting the property attracts £625 pcm. which set against £90,000 (purchase price plus £5000) gives a yield of 8.3%

Not only has the yield been improved but you are likely to get a better quality tenant who is possibly likely to stay for longer.

If you are buying a number of properties and investing a considerable amount of money then take a moment and work out the value of that 0.6% yield that you have created out of thin air! Just on that example you are earning an additional £540 per year.

Now the foregoing has made the system look relatively simple in that you just buy a property, spend some money on improvements and receive a disproportionate increase in income.

Aside from the reasons mentioned above, the reason this scheme is so popular is the fact that a refurbished property is likely to have a greater value and so there is an equity advantage too. This is particularly useful for those investors who wish to remortgage their properties and draw on the equity for future purchases.

In order to ensure that this works for you, you need to be aware of several things. Firstly you cannot overpay for the property in the first place. By using the triangle you should come up with the correct figure as you will base your offer on the rental that the property will currently achieve, not the rent that it could achieve once improved.

Secondly you must be sure that the improvements that you propose will make a positive difference to the rent that is achievable. There are no hard and fast rules in this respect and indeed the correct answer will depend on your local marketplace however the sort of improvements that will generally increase the rental value are as follows:

Neutral Redecoration
Recarpeting
Tidying of Gardens
New worktops
Modern Kitchen/bathrooms

Efficient heating systems
Double-glazing
Creation of an additional bedroom either by subdivision, loft conversion etc.
Creation of off street parking

This is not an exhaustive list but I think you get the idea. Generally speaking major works such as extensions, Garages and the like will often not add enough to the rental income to be worthwhile spends. Remember we are looking to maximise rent not value. An extension may only be the perfect idea if you are planning to buy, refurbish and sell.

The types of improvements that are unlikely to improve the rental value are:

Installation of Sauna
Replacement of parking with a garden
Any poor quality DIY improvements

The final piece of knowledge that you will require is the knowledge of the rough costs of these works. You will need a good idea of the costs of each of these works so that you can have an idea in terms of what you could do to maximise the rent without breaking your budget as well as being able to discern what return on investment you could gain from the improvements.

This will generally come with practice and whilst costs will vary from area to area to follow are the costs that I generally work with:

Assuming a 2 bedroom terrace house:
Carpets   £800.00

Boiler Change	£2,000.00
Replacement Bathroom	£1500.00
Replacement Kitchen	£1800.00
Redecoration	£650.00

Unless you are very skilled in this area you are likely to need to engage the services of professional contractors.

I have been dealing with contractors for many years and can confirm that there are some very good ones and then there are some that are really far more trouble than they are worth. I have seen people work with enormous skill and gusto whilst at the other end of the spectrum I once found a contractor asleep on the floor of the room he was being paid to decorate!

Coincidentally, the vast majority of contractors that I use are actually landlords. Coincidentally, as I didn't know this when I first engaged them but perhaps not coincidentally as that is presumably why they understand what I am trying to achieve and understand the importance of quick responses, courtesy to my tenants and an efficient service.

It is imperative to get the right contractors. You have to strike the balance between cost effectiveness and standard of work and you then need people who are responsible, reliable, polite and hard working. Many people instruct a managing agent to look after their tenancies solely so they can benefit from their contractor relationships.

Whether this is worthwhile or not is a consideration you will have to make your mind up on but consider the following. Let's assume that you manage your property yourself and a tenant calls at 2am in the morning and says they have water running through the building. How long would it be until you could get a plumber round to that property? If it's much more than an hour there could be serious damage to the property. My answer to this question would be fifteen minutes. How do I know? – because it happened to me a short while ago and my contractor arrived just inside quarter of an hour.

You need to ensure that your contractors work to the required timescale and on budget as overruns will come straight off your yield and therefore should be avoided at all costs. If you are not used to dealing with contractors then it is certainly worthwhile to consider employing a project manager for larger works. The charge is typically 10% of the contract value but they will be on site ensuring the work is to standard required and that the schedule is being adhered too. They could be a real lifesaver.

You must ensure that any contractors you engage have a good knowledge of planning and building regulations requirements. Always enquire whether the works you want carried out will require building regulation consent, planning permission, listed building consent or any other permissions. The last thing you want to do is get works undertaken only to find that they are non compliant with some regulations and you have to start again. To do so will in all likelihood completely obliterate any profit the development would have given you and that's quite apart from the free labour you may have put into the project!

The phrase "failing to plan is planning to fail" can be a sore lesson in the world of property!

The next chapter assumes that as a prospective long term property investor you elect to let the property.

CHAPTER 8
GETTING THE PROPERTY READY FOR LETTING.

Never, Never, Never give up.
Winston Churchill.

This part of the process is important as if you give up now then you will never reap the rewards of your hard work thus far.

Assuming you are holding the property for long term rental, one of the first decisions you will need to make is whether you are going to undertake the letting and management of the property yourself or whether you are planning on appointing an Agent.

For those who decide against a letting agent managing their portfolio and whom intend on maintaining a full time job elsewhere, thought should be given before allowing a portfolio to become too large. My personal view is that around 10 units is the maximum possible you can effectively manage whilst also maintaining a full time job. This advice should obviously be tempered with the fact that an HMO will take up far more time and administration than a corporate let!

Self Managed or Managed by an agent:

This is a question that has been debated for as many years as I have been in the industry. The statistics are mixed in that around 50% of Buy to Let property is managed by an agent and the remaining approximately 50% is self-managed by the landlord.

Having owned a chain of estate agency offices myself, I am clearly going to champion the need to use a professional managing agent but in the following paragraphs I shall set out my understanding of this conundrum in order that you can make a decision for yourself.

Given this book is all about a calculation which will assist you, why not add another calculation just for fun? For this one I ask you to work out your hourly rate from your current employment.

The average hourly rate for someone on the average national salary of £22,500 and working a 40 hour week is £10.82 gross. The average rent in the UK is currently around £750 and therefore at 10% the agents' average fee is £75.00 per month.

If you are spending more than 7 hours a month on your property then you are spending more of your own time than it would cost you to employ a managing agent. If the rent of your property is £400 or £500 per month then you surely cannot be better off self-managing.

If the above has not convinced you then consider the benefits in using a managing agent. Firstly and most importantly they are more likely to find you a better tenant. Bad tenants will avoid letting agents as they know they will be thoroughly referenced. Those tenants who apply to a landlord via a private advert normally get themselves in on the basis of a single meeting and without any robust background checks.

It is likely that the agent has better access to a better range of skilled tradesmen who can undertake repairs and the like at your property more promptly and possibly more cost effectively than those contractors you could source yourself. The tenant is likely to be happier due to a faster response time and the fact that they have a point of contact of your agent to raise any issues often before they become major issues.

Additionally the agent will be able to advise you in terms of demand to allow you to set a realistic rent level for your property and to increase the rent where the market will support it. This information is worth the management fee on its own but bear in mind also that the agent is likely to be able to negotiate more successfully than you could probably do yourself.

A further advantage is that if you have an ongoing relationship with an agent, you are more likely to be offered property for sale when it comes available. The agent is far more likely to want to sell you a property that they will get back for letting and management than they would to someone who undertakes this function themselves. It's simple economics when you think about it – the problem is that a lot of landlords do not think about it!

If you are still not convinced then consider the fact that there are around 70 pieces of legislation surrounding landlord and tenant matters and the law is changing all the time. Unless you make time to familiarize yourself with the legislation and any amendments to it, you are quite likely to make a mistake or not be best equipped in certain circumstances. Your agent, on the other hand, would be able to guide you through the legislation and ensure that you stay the right side of the law.

You may also find that your mortgage lender requires that the property is managed by a letting agent and where this is a condition of the loan, you should ensure that the agent you wish to appoint is a member of whichever regulatory body the lender requests. This will normally be ARLA (Association of Residential Letting Agents) or the RICS (Royal Institution of Chartered Surveyors.)

Self-Management:
Many property investors manage their own properties and provided they have a good working knowledge of landlord and tenant matters there is potentially little wrong with this.

My personal point of view is that investors would be better suited to have someone manage the tenancies. They generally take up a disproportionate amount of time which could be more profitably spent on revenue generating activities.

It is also true that a third party could be a little more canny with deciphering the difference between a wish list and required maintenance. It is often the case when you know the tenant and they know that you hold the purse strings that they can get more done than is actually necessary.

By using an agent the tenancy is run on a more commercial basis. I am confident that the value I get from the agents I use is far in excess of the fees that they charge. They are also better equipped to respond to emergency issues than I could be myself.

Remember that management fees are tax deductible and managed tenancies tend to be longer than unmanaged ones.

Additionally it may be worth noting that a letting agent may put more effort into securing a tenant for a managed property than for a let only one. Further they are less likely to give you a duff tenant given that it is they who will need to manage that individual and collect their rent. The increased speed of the let and subconscious additional screening probably on their own justify the agents annual management charges!

Many landlords who self manage do so following a poor experience with a letting agent. I appreciate, as with every industry, there are good agents and there are very bad agents. A bad agent will do nothing for the longevity of the tenancy and will do nothing to work the relationship with the tenant. In such circumstances I too would self manage. However there are some amazing managing agents out there and once you find one you will truly wonder why you ever considered trying to manage your portfolio yourself.

In summation the only advantage to not using a professional managing agent is the cost saving which once an allowance for tax has been made and an understanding of the cost of your own time is probably not a saving at all!

Finding a tenant:
There are a number of methods that you can use to find a tenant however regardless of how you undertake this task please ensure that your selection strategy is thorough. As a director of a firm which undertakes tenant evictions, I can confirm that there are all sorts of tricks that prospective tenants will try in order to get into your property! Over the years our referencing division has seen forged payslips, bogus employer references and everything inbetween!

The first thing you need to do is decide whether you wish to use a tenant referencing firm or whether you want to undertake the referencing yourself. I hope you have already realised that not doing any referencing at all is a really bad idea!

Before deciding you should have a read of any mortgage conditions you have if the property is mortgaged as it may stipulate that the tenant is referenced by an acknowledged tenant reference firm. It would also be prudent to check the details of your building insurance policy for the same purpose.

This research will also likely tell you whether you are permitted to rent to those in receipt of housing benefit, DSS referrals from the local authority and the like. Please ensure you comply with your mortgage and insurers conditions. There is no upside to subsequently finding you are in breach!

If you have elected to use one of the professional tenant referencing firms then the process is likely to be as follows. The tenant completes an online form with all their details and the referencing firm set about contacting employers, landlords and credit reference agencies to verify the information they have been given.

The reports are generally not expensive at around £15 and provided the report does not uncover anything negative you can normally obtain rent guarantee cover and/or cover against the costs in the event that the tenant needs to be evicted should you wish.

Once the report is completed the landlord will be sent a copy. This final report should include confirmation from the landlord whether the rent has been paid on time, confirmation from the employer about your tenants income and details whether or not the employment is temporary or whether the applicant is at risk of redundancy and further it should include some credit information.

Some landlords are looking to reject applicants who work on zero hours contracts but I personally think this is a bridge too far. Whilst they do not have guaranteed hours the same could be said for someone who is self employed. I think the key is to see what their income has been over the last 6 – 12 months and then assess the likelihood of this changing. Whilst it pays to be thorough when it comes to tenant referencing, if you were to reject anyone who was self employed or on a zero hours contract you would effectively be removing several million people who may have otherwise happily taken your property!

The credit information is actually very interesting. Whilst I appreciate that many people simply look at the credit score and whether the tenant has any adverse entries such as County Court Judgments, I always look at the information to gauge the tenants attitude to money. If the tenant has applied for lots of credit in the recent past it may be illustrative that they are living beyond their means, for those who regularly close and open bank accounts they may be doing so to avoid actions by creditors.

Some landlords I know also ask to have a look at the tenants' bank statements to see how they live and what they spend their money on. Whilst I personally feel this to be a little intrusive I can see the merit in it. For example tenants who have lots of payments to payday loan companies will generally be living above their means.

Some landlords also insist on a home visit where they or their agent will visit the tenant in their existing home to assess how clean and tidy it is and to what extent they look after a landlords' property. Critics of this often state that because the tenant knows when the visit is they will clean the property and so the landlord will learn nothing. I disagree. If the tenants idea of cleanliness is non existent then their efforts at presenting a clean home will fail.

So now the tenant has been selected and referenced you need to get the property ready for their move in...

There is a lot to do to get the property ready for letting but getting it right at the outset will save on headaches later on. For those novice in investing I would suggest you make yourself a checklist covering the following points and you can tick them off as you go. Aside from ensuring you have everything covered there will be a real sense of achievement once they are all ticked and you can get the tenant moved in!

Firstly you should check that everything works at the property. Does the toilet flush?, are there keys for the window locks?, do the doors open and close freely?, does the cooker and extractor hood work?, does the washing machine drain away properly?, are there light bulbs in each room?

Whilst these may seem like trivial things, they mean a great deal to tenants and when discovered on a stressful move in day, their reaction on finding any issues may be a little disproportionate! If you imagine the disappointment you would experience if you arrived on holiday to a hotel suite to find that it wasn't clean, there were no towels and the TV was broken.

My advice is to always allow at least a days grace before you move a tenant in. That way you have enough time to check these things and ensure the move in goes to plan.

Aside from these, there are some other important property related issues which must be attended to prior to the tenancy starting.

One of the most important legislative requirements for properties with a gas supply is the provision of a valid gas safety certificate. These are a legal requirement and are valid for 12 months. The engineer who undertakes the inspection should be registered on the Gas Safe Register and have approval for the type of heating system that is installed at your property. In short, if you haven't got a valid gas safety certificate then the tenant cannot move in!

The electrical installation should also be checked by a competent person to ensure it is correctly operating and above all safe. Advice on this point appears to vary although many commentators suggest that the electrical installation be inspected at least once every five years. For those of you who are offering furnished accommodation you will need to have PAT (portable appliance testing) carried out by an electrician for every appliance that is included in the letting including but not limited to kettles, toasters, washing machines, TVs, DVD players, lamps and the like. Generally speaking, if it has a plug on it then it needs to be PAT tested.

More recent legislation requires landlords to have conducted a Legionella survey in their property to try and identify any risk of this disease. A number of firms have appeared over the last couple of years that will undertake this inspection and charges seem to be in the region of around £150.00. Once the report has been carried out there is a requirement to monitor the situation on an ongoing basis.

Another property requirement prior to the letting of the property is to provide the tenant with a copy of the Energy Performance Certificate (EPC) for the property. This document sets out the energy efficiency of the property both currently as well as detailing the level of efficiency which could be enjoyed in the event that various improvements were undertaken.

Currently there is no obligation for landlords to improve the energy rating of their properties (although legislation is on its way in this regard) but there is a requirement that the tenant receive a copy of the certificate.

A good number of properties have already been surveyed and you can see if yours has by visiting www.epcregister.com. The certificate lasts 10 years for properties that are to be rented. Bear in mind if you have just purchased your investment property, the seller should have provided a copy of the EPC to your solicitor as part of the sales documentation.

I am assuming that you have by now had the tenant properly referenced and are happy with the results obtained. The property is now ready for occupation and compliant in respect of the various checks that are required. That being the case it's now time to get the tenant into your property.

So now you are on the cusp of being able to collect some rent, to follow are the documents that you should produce when signing up your new tenant.

Move in Day:
The first key document that is required is the Tenancy Agreement. This is basically the contract between you as the landlord and your tenant. It will include all the salient details of the arrangement such as the property address, the dates the tenancy is for, the amount of rent, the amount of deposit and an address for service for the landlord. I have seen tenancies of two or three pages and I have seen the governments new suggestion of a tenancy, which I recall, runs to around 30

pages. Regardless of which you decide to use, provided the correct details are in there then it should be enforceable.

If you are having a Guarantor to support the tenancy then this can be included either as part of the tenancy agreement or alternatively by way of a separate guarantor agreement. There is no right answer in terms of how you should construct it although my personal preference is to include the tenants and the guarantor in one tenancy agreement document which all of the parties sign. My reason for saying this is not only will it avoid problems if the guarantor agreement was to get lost but will also cover in the event that the guarantor subsequently says that they were unsure of what they were guaranteeing given that they had not received/signed the tenancy agreement. There is also an argument that the guarantor could suggest their guarantee is invalid in that they signed it prior to the tenancy commencing. All these arguments could be avoided in the event that there is one document. I even go so far as to get the guarantor to initial by each covenant in the tenancy which relates to the guarantor.

So the tenancy needs to be signed by the tenant and any guarantor. Incidentally you can have a verbal tenancy but this is not recommended.

I would suggest that as well as signing at the end of the tenancy the parties initial each page of the document. You don't want arguments later where you are accused of adding or removing pages of the tenancy after it was originally signed and for the sake of a few sets of initials this can be avoided.

My advice is that you also get the tenants to sign a disclaimer regarding the utility supplies at the property. Historically the landlord could have set up the utility accounts for their tenants and indeed many letting agents used to do so. Then along came the Data Protection Act and that opportunity was lost forever. Nowadays landlords can only hope that their tenants set up utility accounts in their own names once they have moved into a property but I have heard of plenty of cases where this has not been the case and the landlord gets a charming letter from the utility company sometimes months after the tenants have left.

The tenancy will detail that the tenants are liable for the consumption of any utilities at the property but it is useful to have a document which confirms that the tenant will indemnify the landlord in the event that the tenants do not set up the accounts in their own names. To assist the tenants in this respect my utility document includes the contact numbers of the various utility companies and council tax office together with the address and postcode of the property which will obviously be required when they call to set up their accounts.

More recently a few firms have sprung up who offer landlords and letting agents a service whereby they will contact the tenant for you discuss the energy options available to them and get their accounts set up. Provided the tenant has given you consent to release their details to such a third party it sounds like a superb idea particularly given I understand the service is free and is funded by way of a referral payment from the utility providers themselves. This is not a service I have used personally but I would certainly be receptive to doing so in the future.

The next document in your bundle should be the property inventory. With the current tenant deposit legislation and a generally more litigious environment in which we all now live, this is an incredibly important document.

The inventory should not be a collage of the pretty photos you used to advertise the property to let but should instead be a thorough written and photographic (and video if you wish) record of the condition of the property at the outset of the tenancy. As a guide to thoroughness for an unfurnished 2 bedroom flat I would expect to have around 40 photographs. A general rule of thumb is to take six pictures per room. One from each corner of the room and one directed to the floor and one directed to the ceiling. In kitchens you should include a photo of the hob, sink and inside of the cooker whilst a bathroom should have a photo of the bath, inside the WC and the basin. Also ensure you do one of the garden too as tenants have a habit of leaving a property when the grass is about a foot tall!

It may sound like overkill but you will be grateful of it in the event of a dispute at the end of the tenancy. Consider some examples for a moment. You want to deduct from the deposit the cost of repainting the ceiling as it is nicotine stained from a smoker. It is now off white rather than the brilliant white it was at the start of the tenancy. Without photos you would be unable to prove it is any different. The iron burn in the carpet – that wasn't there at the start or was it? See, you are grateful of that carpet photograph now!

The photographs should be accompanied by a written record of the property known often as the schedule of condition. It should note any existing defects which are there at the start of the tenancy such as "chip on worktop next to sink", cracked tile in bathroom just above wash basin" and the like.

Instead of preparing this yourself you may wish to engage the services of a professional inventory provider. Most are

144

members of their professional organisation and will have APIP after their names. Professional inventories tend to start at around £100.

Tenants should be comfortable to sign these documents as not only are they signing to acknowledge the state of the property when they take it on they are also being given assurances that they will not be blamed for, or charged for any pre existing defects.

In addition you should provide the tenant with a copy of the gas safety certificate and a copy of the energy performance certificate. To avoid any suggestions that you may have overlooked this, it is good practice to get them to sign a copy which you can keep on your file.

The final document, which is an essential part of the move in bundle, is the deposit information (assuming you are taking a deposit). There is legislation surrounding this and so if you are suitably interested you could head for section 212 of the 2004 Housing Act. In simple terms if you are taking a deposit then you are obliged to lodge it with one of the three government approved schemes within 30 days of receiving it.

In addition you are obliged to serve the tenant what is known as "prescribed information" which is basically a document which details the tenants details, property details together with the details of the scheme in which the deposit is being protected. Appended to that should be the terms and conditions of that deposit scheme which are generally downloadable from their respective website.

Whilst there is no obligation for the tenant to sign these documents it is doubtless the easiest way to subsequently prove that they not only received them but also received them within the required time limits, so make sure they are in your move in bundle.

So now you have a signed tenancy, signed utilities document, signed inventory and schedule of condition, signed gas safety certificate and EPC together with the signed prescribed information relating to the deposit. Now the fun bit – take their money!

It is standard practice that the tenant pays the first months rent in advance and the deposit prior to signing the tenancy and receiving the keys. Alarm bells should ring if your prospective tenant is struggling to get the move in monies together – it does not bode well for how they may conduct the tenancy.

Good practice at this stage would be to try and get the tenant to sign a standing order form in respect of the second and subsequent months rental monies.

Once this is all done then hand over the keys and you can now start looking for your next property investment!

During the tenancy:
Clearly as a landlord you are going to have to arrange for the routine repair and renewal of the various bits and pieces at your property which may break, fall off or disappear but it is important that even if you do not make a visit for a repair at the request of the tenant that you do make regular inspections of your property. Sensibly this should probably be every six months.

The reason for this is that you will be on the look out for problems and issues which your tenant may not have been aware of or made you aware of.

To put this in context most tenants will only report issues to you that are causing them a problem or some inconvenience. So if the boiler fails and there is no hot water then you will certainly get a call from your tenant. Similarly if the cold tap is dripping at night and keeping them awake, you will probably get a call. The issue arises when there is a matter of disrepair which does not immediately cause them an inconvenience but could, if left unattended to, cause damage to the building and become a very costly item to deal with.

One example could be the washing machine pipe that is dripping. The washing machine works fine and so the tenant does not complain but the incessant dripping could end up causing wood rot to the floor and then damage to the skirting boards, joists – I think you get the picture. So when you undertake periodic inspections look for these things, dripping pipes, a leaky radiator, overflowing guttering, loose roof tiles and poor pointing to brickwork. Remember this is your investment and you need to preserve its value. Failure to undertake simple routine tasks could lead to costly repair bills in the future. For that reason a periodic inspection of the property is very important.

Aside from your periodic inspections, do remember that the gas appliances will need checking by a gas safe engineer every year and it is advisable to have the electrical system inspected and tested at least once every five years.

The other important facet during a tenancy is of course the collection of the rent! Whilst landlords should act reasonably and provide some latitude, my experience is that you should remain reasonably strict in terms of rent payments. The other lesson I have learned is that deteriorating rent situations rarely rectify themselves and therefore early action is considered prudent to avoid further losses.

Many tenants will be happy to pay by standing order direct to your account and depending on your preference this is probably the easiest method to work with. Do however remember to check each month that the rent is appearing, do not assume it has just because you haven't heard to the contrary. You would be staggered to learn of the number of eviction cases my firm have been involved in where the landlord didn't realise that the rent had stopped for, in some cases, over a year. Once the rent is that heavily in arrears the chances of bringing the tenancy back on track are greatly diminished and for most landlords eviction is the only option.

Some of you may take tenants who are in receipt of Housing Benefit. It is important to bear in mind that Housing benefit is generally paid four weekly in arrears rather than the calendar month in advance that the tenancy states it is due. This differential needs to be carefully managed on the basis that the tenancy requires 12 monthly payments in advance each year yet the housing benefit department of the council will be paying 13 payments in arrears each year.

Care should also be exercised to ensure that any housing benefit claim remains in pay. In this respect good lines of communication are required with your tenant as the local authority will periodically require them to provide information relating to their benefit entitlement. If they fail to provide this information in a timely fashion then their housing benefit claim could be suspended. Bear in mind that if the payment is coming directly to you as the landlord there is far less incentive for the tenant to act in a timely fashion and therefore it is critical you try and maintain a positive relationship with all your tenants but especially perhaps those in receipt of a housing benefit award.

Bringing a tenancy to an end:
As the saying goes "all good things must come to an end" and tenancies are no different. Whether they have gone well or not they will, at some stage, come to an end.

It is important to bear in mind that a tenancy can come to an end in one of two ways. Technically there is a third way but the law of frustration is slightly beyond the remit of this book. In essence therefore a tenancy can end either by its surrender by the tenant or where the landlord has obtained an order for possession from the County Court.

In all other circumstances there is a risk that a tenant could claim that they have been unlawfully evicted and the penalties of this are far reaching. Landlords should also be aware of the suggestions that a tenancy can end if the tenant abandons the property or where the landlord places a notice on the front door, the so called "Abandonment Notice." There is nothing in landlord and tenant law which acknowledges the concept of abandonment and therefore it should not be used.

Surrender of the tenancy works on the basis that the tenant voluntarily ends the tenancy. This could be by them giving notice that they are going to leave and then subsequently returning the keys or even without giving notice and simply returning the keys to the landlord. Technically such action is an offer to surrender by the tenant but it normally leaves little scope for the landlord to negotiate!

Where a tenant has not surrendered their keys but you feel that they have moved out you should always end the tenancy in the formal way. To not do so may put you at risk of unlawful eviction in the event that the tenant returns and decides they want to continue to live there. This is true regardless of whether their rent account is up to date or not.

Whilst I am not going to go into huge detail about tenancy law in this section (I may keep that for another book!) the process in very simple terms works on the following basis.

If the tenant has done nothing wrong and you want to bring the tenancy to an end then the normal course of action would be to serve what is known as a Section 21 Notice. In the event that the tenant is in breach of their tenancy, for example they have not paid their rent, then the normal course of action would be to serve what is called a Section 8 Notice. The section 21 Notice does not require the landlord to give a reason why they want their property back but the Section 8 Notice must specify the grounds (i.e. breaches of tenancy) that the landlord is going to rely upon in order to try and gain possession of the property.

Once the notices expire, in the event that the tenant has not left the property then you are obliged to file a claim in the County Court local to the property to enforce that notice and to try and gain possession of the property.

Once this claim is filed with the Court there is normally a short court hearing in front of the District Judge (except for some Section 21 claims which do not always require a hearing).

The Judge will ask some questions at the hearing and peruse the documentation that has been supplied to them. In the event that they are satisfied that the landlord should have their property back then they will make an order that the tenant leave on a set date which is normally 14 days (but can be up to 42 days) from the date of the court hearing.

The order for possession will normally also include an order that the tenant pay the court fee that has been incurred by the landlord and in the event that you have followed the Section 8 route in respect of rent arrears, the order may also include an order for the payment of the rent owed to the landlord.

My experience is that recovery of these sums from tenants is far from guaranteed. The old adage "you can't get blood out of a stone" is true here and before you spend more money on debt recovery services, give some thought to the financial standing of your tenant and any guarantor and assess what likelihood there is that they could pay. A sensible alternative is to perhaps consider engaging someone on a "no collect - no fee" basis. Something could be better than nothing.

The piece of paper containing the Judges order is what is known as the order for possession. In the event that the tenant does not vacate on the date set by the Judge then the landlord must make a further application to the court for the warrant of possession. This is basically an instruction for the County Court Bailiff to enforce the order for possession and get the property back for the landlord.

The time delays of the court system and the bailiff, particularly during periods where the tenant has stopped paying rent, can be frustrating but please do not be tempted to follow an alternative path.

Without wanting to alarm you, one case which went before the courts involved a landlord who obtained a possession order against his tenant but, in between obtaining that and arranging for the tenant to be evicted via the County Court Bailiff, he decided to evict the tenant himself. The fines imposed on the landlord totalled almost £10,000. In the event that he had just obtained the warrant of possession and waited for that to be executed by the County Court Bailiff his cost would have simply been the court fee of £110.

If you are going to be a buy to let investor then you must remember this: If you are wanting to bring a tenancy to an end then follow the correct channels and do not deviate from them. If you are unsure of how it should be done then employ a professional firm. If you try it and get it wrong the consequences could be very costly!

I apologise to any readers in Scotland or Northern Ireland as the above details the eviction process for England and Wales only. Scotland is slightly different and Northern Ireland is very different.

CHAPTER 9
MAKING IT A CAREER.

If you don't drive your business then you will be driven out of business.
B.C. Forbes.

For many of you, acquiring just one buy to let or investment property will be enough for you and for those looking to trade, perhaps one at a time is enough. But doubtless some of you will be so enthused having read this book that you will be wanting to pen up your resignation letter to your employer and make property your full time career!

It may well be right for you to take the plunge and become a property person, indeed as someone once said, *"If you don't take risks then you will always work for someone who does."*

In considering your career, it is also worth mentioning that property investment could be a solitary alternative to your current employment. Investors generally work on their own or certainly in small groups and it is rare, certainly in the early days, to have a pretty office filled with staff, water dispensers and free post-it notes. All jokes aside, you should consider how you would feel working on your own, without the comradery of your current work colleagues and without the pseudo guarantee of a salary at the end of each month.

From a personal point of view I thoroughly enjoyed working in my estate agency offices. I never adopted a private office room, always preferring to be in the thick of the front office activity. It is quite a change to now spend at least half of my working day on my own. I don't regret it but these are all things you should think of before you take the plunge.

Additionally you should consider how you will motivate yourself. With a "normal" job there is the requirement to get up and get to the office for 8.45am and remain there until 6, or whatever your hours may be. As a self-employed person there is no obligation to be at your desk and if you are the sort of person who could be easily distracted by breakfast television then this could be a challenge for you.

Thankfully I am pretty committed to what I am doing and so lay ins are reserved for the weekends. After all, after 20 years of working Saturdays in the estate agency I figure I am due a few weekend lay ins now!

If property is going to be your chosen profession then like any other you need to get organised and equipped so that you can be a success at it. As with so many other callings in life you will need the support of those around you and never more so is this the case than with property.

To follow is a brief run down of the personnel that you should seek to have at your disposal. The great thing about property investment is that you are unlikely to need to employ any of them on a full time basis but simply to engage their services as and when the need arises. It is however critical that you have people in place that you can trust who are effective, efficient and can get the job done. After all your reputation as an investor will depend on it.

Much has been said about the need for people to assist you in the property journey and whilst I personally dislike the pseudo

Americanism of "Power team" it does aptly describe what is required.

In order to have credibility and the ability to progress in property investment, there are a few individuals who you will need to work with and we shall consider them as follows:

Solicitor/Licensed Conveyancer:
Property transactions need to be created by deed and therefore there is an advantage to use a solicitor or licensed conveyancer. Indeed if you are purchasing with a mortgage you are going to need to use a solicitor/conveyancer that is approved by the mortgage lender. As a property investor you need a solicitor who will perform two functions. The first is that of the property transfer and all the legal elements of purchasing a property. The second equally important factor is their ability to willingly liaise with the agent and any other third party through which you are buying the property to get the deal done in the timescale that is required.

You would be absolutely amazed at the number of solicitors who do not speak to agents or who treat agents as an inconvenience and who can drag a simple transaction out for 3 months or more. If you are to make any positive relationships with the local agents this simply will not do. You want a solicitor who will do what is required and get a deal done in no more than 28 days.

I recently saw a posting on the Internet from a law firm where they were moaning that they don't like instructions from estate agents as they have to liaise with them for which they do not get remunerated and have to transfer their commission fee to them upon completion; a transfer for which they get charged for. It amazed me as nowhere in the post did they acknowledge that probably the lions share of their work is referral work from estate agents which must save them thousands of pounds in advertising and marketing costs which they would incur if no one referred work to them.

In my opinion, it is absolutely worthwhile paying the extra for the right one. If you got the chance to purchase a property at 20% below its real value on the basis you can conclude the purchase within a month, it is a false economy to lose that deal because you wanted to save a few pounds and use a cheaper solicitor.

I have used the same solicitor for around 10 years and whilst he professes that I get a "Graham Kinnear" discount, I know that I could get conveyancing done for less than he charges me. What I couldn't get elsewhere is the level of service, efficiency and effort that he puts in to ensure that I get my transaction through as quickly as is possible and with the minimum of fuss. Aside from that he is a thoroughly nice chap and in my world that also counts for something.

Indeed on occasions I have offered to pay the solicitors fees for the seller on the basis that I can direct who they use for conveyancing. For such circumstances I have another superb chap who is a partner in a law firm. He is a former estate agent himself and so he understands completely what I am trying to achieve.

I would exercise caution using the solicitor suggested by the selling agent. The advantage, where there are multiple offers on a property, could be that the agent favours your offer, if you are going to use their solicitor, as they will earn more out of the transaction but the disadvantage is that you could be signing up to a low cost call centre type of operation where part of the solicitors fee goes to the agent for the referral and leaves less for the solicitor to provide you with a superb service.

In the past I have addressed this conundrum by saying to the agent that as part of my offer I will pay them what they would have received if I had used their solicitor but then used my own. This way the agent gets their money, the transaction goes through smoothly with a solicitor I trust and the job is done. If the property can yield you say a £10,000 profit the day you buy it then why lose out for the sake of a couple of hundred pounds?

Letting Agent:
A good quality letting agent is worth their weight in gold. A professional agent can provide you with accurate information in terms of what a property could potentially let for and also guide you in terms of the standard that you should attain in order to attract the calibre of tenant that you are looking for. Their intense knowledge of the local letting market will allow them to assist you to maximise your property investment. My advice with letting agents is not to haggle on their fees. Assuming you pick correctly, the agent will generally far exceed their quoted service offering and they are worth well in excess of the 10% of rent collected that they normally charge. Their ability to screen tenants and work relationships with tenants will minimise void periods and maximise the longevity of a tenancy which will benefit you far more greatly than a 10% reduction in their fees could ever achieve.

If you can work your way to a preferred landlord status with an agent then you may well get the first opportunity to buy property their agency arm may be selling as they will know that you will retain them to let the property that you buy. If you don't use the letting agency arm of your estate agent then it is

157

hardly surprising that the landlords who do will be the ones who are initially offered the investment property that they are instructed to sell.

Another top tip for dealing with letting agents is to never ever blame them for the actions of the tenants. The letting agent is there to find the tenant and to manage the tenancy. They have no control of whether the tenant gives the correct notice, whether the tenant doesn't clean when they leave or whether the tenant leaves their 6ft python in the flat when they move out. Work with your letting agent and not against them. You are both on the same side. Ask any letting agent who their favourite clients are and you will be told that the ones they favour are the ones who are professional landlords, who do what they say they are going to do and support the agent in their efforts. Those who are always seeking to blame an agent for something that is outside of their control are unlikely to get the first call when an investment property becomes available. Regardless, the old adage of "together we are stronger" is certainly true in terms of working with your agent. Demonstrate loyalty and appreciation with them and the rewards will be clear to see.

There are many ways you can try and select a letting agent but my view is that you should select someone you feel you can work with on a day to day basis. Never more true is the old adage "People buy People" and so find someone you think you connect with.

Notwithstanding that there are some questions you should really be clear on before you sign that agency agreement.

Firstly as of 1 October 2014 the agent must be a member of one of the three government redress schemes. It is now a legal requirement and failure to register would leave the agency open to a fine of £5,000.

Secondly the agency should have a protection scheme in place for its Client monies to ensure that in the event of the failure of the lettings business any rents and/or tenant deposits are not lost.

Thirdly you may want to consider using an agent which is affiliated to one of the national bodies such as ARLA (Association of Residential Letting Agents.) Whilst not a guarantee of good practice it does show that the agency has the intention and desire to offer a professional and transparent service.

Finally see if you can meet all of the letting and management team before you instruct an agent. If you place your properties in the hands of one individual then you will have an issue if they leave and move to another firm.

Estate Agent:
If your goal is to trade property, then it is important that you have a good relationship with an effective sales agent. It matters not whether they work for an independent or one of the corporate chains. What counts is the ability to work with them and them to have the skill, commitment and determination to get your property sold for the best price in the shortest period of time.

For your first property sale have a few agents out to visit the property and try and gauge their enthusiasm levels, try to gauge the reach of their marketing and see how comfortable they are at the proposed marketing price. If the agent does not believe he can achieve the asking price you are after it is likely to be a self-fulfilling prophecy! Notwithstanding be wary of the agent who may try and overvalue the property just to get the listing on their books!

Alternatively you could try and source some recommendations from other property investors you may have met at network meetings and the like. Having been an agent myself I truly believe a good agent is worth their weight in gold.

Mortgage broker:
Assuming you need finance for your investments, Mortgage Brokers are another key member of your team. You should establish a relationship with a mortgage broker who, in addition to having access to the entire marketplace has a good deal of experience not only with Buy to Let and Commercial Funding but also the type of property that you are looking to acquire.

There is little point engaging a mortgage broker who has little or no experience in dealing with funding for houses in multiple occupation if your intention is to build a portfolio of multi let student property. Further, there is no point in using a broker with no experience of selective licensing in the event that you are wanting to invest in an area which is covered by such a scheme.

Speak to a few brokers and get a feel for how they understand what you need to achieve.

I use an independent broker and have done for over a decade. The lady I use is incredibly approachable, accessible and tireless in her efforts to get a deal placed. Once the application is in progress she will relentlessly chase the lender until the mortgage offer is issued. Such tenacity is essential to ensure that you get the deal you have searched so hard for. Again – there is no point trying to save a couple of hundred pounds on a brokers fee only to find that their delays cost you the £20,000 profit that the property purchase could have instantly made you.

Surveyor:
If you are using mortgage finance then the lender you use will send a valuer to have a look at the property. Be under no illusion, this is not a survey. It is normally paid for by you but is entirely for the benefit of the lender to ensure, firstly that the property exists and that the mortgage application is not a fraudulent one and secondly to assess the suitability of that property for secured lending purposes.

For many investors, including myself, that is enough but you should give serious consideration in commissioning a more thorough survey particularly if you have not got a property background. A more thorough survey may reveal issues which are costly to rectify and by highlighting them before you commit to the purchase it will give you the opportunity to withdraw from the transaction if the issues warrant such a draconian move or to renegotiate the price if this is warranted. Without the survey you could buy a property with major structural defects which you may be unable to sell or let until the remedial works are carried out.

Surveyors can also be a useful source of property. Many surveyors are asked to look at property that may be being repossessed by banks long before it actually comes to the market. It is therefore possible to gain a "heads up" from such individuals of properties which may be coming to the market and give you, in the right circumstances, the opportunity to buy them before anyone else does.

Builder/Contractor:
A builder or contractor is absolutely essential unless you live very close to your properties and are pretty adept in the art of DIY.

One key way of promoting the longevity of a tenancy is to attend quickly to issues of maintenance and repair. In the event that you engage a letting agent to manage the tenancy they will generally have access to a team of tradespeople who can undertake these functions. For those who self manage you will need to ensure that you have this area covered. Avid DIY fans should be aware that they should leave electrics and Gas well alone and instead use a Part P qualified electrician and Gas safe Registered Gas Engineer to ensure they stay the right side of the law.

It is unacceptable for a tenant to be left a fortnight without heating, a shower or other basic amenity. It is critical for the relationship and the success of the tenancy that repairs and planned maintenance take place in a timely fashion.

This concludes the members of your initial team however for those of you who end up getting involved in more complex deals and transactions you may also need to look at some of the following:

Architect:
There are many people who trade as architects and a chartered architect will be a member of the Royal Institution of British Architects. Aside from this band of highly qualified people are architectural consultants who in many instances are very good but are just not qualified chartered architects.

Historically I have used both but it rather depends on the project that you are proposing to undertake. The firm that I use most often undertake a variety of works for me including the creation of lease plans, planning permissions for change of use, consents for subdivision of premises and single new build applications. In the event that I was proposing to build 100 new homes (which I am not!) then it may be that I would use them in conjunction with a larger firm or indeed look to appoint someone different. I suppose the key point here is to ensure that the firm you engage are familiar and experienced in the sort of work that you are wanting to undertake.

Planning Consultant:
Whilst I have never directly engaged a planning consultant I understand they have a valuable role to play. They are concerned with the issues that will be raised when a planning application is considered by the local authority or indeed the secretary of state. They are most commonly used for ambitious or contentious sites and their input can mean a consent can be achieved earlier and with less cost than perhaps would otherwise be the case.

Project Manager:
Project Managers are generally used for schemes where the cost is upwards of £50,000 although they are available for smaller works. It is their role to ensure that the build is going to plan and to standard and that the budget is maintained. They are often Building Surveyors but in my experience they are an essential part of a big build project.

In the event that you are raising finance for a development the lender may even appoint their own project manager (and obviously charge you for the privilege) so that they can be sure

163

of the progress of the works and the standards of the works before they release each stage payment.

If you are planning to undertake development works of this nature it would be good for you to make some introductions early on so that you have some names to consider before you need to start the project.

Lawyer:
Aside from the Solicitor or Conveyancer who is to undertake the transfer of the property from the seller to you or indeed from you to your buyer, you may have a need for a property lawyer.

Amongst their skills could be experience and expertise in boundary disputes, drafting leases, property disputes and things like adverse possession. Whilst unlikely to be an immediate requirement for a novice investor or someone early on in their property career, it would be comforting to know you have some one in mind should the need arise. If you are in search of names then you may wish to start on the Internet. The Law Society website allows you to select law firms from location and area of specialism. Alternatively your conveyancing solicitor may be able to make an appropriate suggestion.

So let's assume you have the aptitude, determination to succeed and a team of people at your disposal to ensure that every eventuality is covered. How do you actually get started?

Well in our business it is all about the property. Buy the right one for the right price and whether you are selling or renting it, you should do well. The trick is to find the properties. We have talked about this in an earlier chapter and there is no single correct answer. To follow are some of the methods that full time investors sometimes use to source stock in addition to the methods we have already talked about:

Website:
You could consider the creation of a website which advertises that you buy property quickly at a discount to market value. Websites can be optimised to appear in better positions in the search engines such as Google and Yahoo and this can be done by organic improvements or alternatively by way of a pay per click advertising scheme. It is not my intention to offer advice as to the success or otherwise that these methods may give you but simply to make you aware of them.

Land Registry:
The land registry is available to everyone and you can search the name and address of the owner of a property. Perhaps it is the case that you drive past a run down property every day on the way to work. Why not track down the owner and see if they want to sell?

I remember dealing with a situation where an investor did just that for a commercial property in Herne Bay in Kent. The lady who owned the property had inherited it and had never seen the property and had never been to Herne Bay. She was delighted at the prospect of selling. The building is now a lovely development of flats and it never went on the open market. The Land Registry therefore represents an easy, inexpensive way of potentially contacting sellers of property you may be interested in.

Social Media.
I am a bit long in the tooth to say that I am a social media expert but I do visit these sites with some regularity. What I have noticed recently is dedicated groups of property people

165

who share thoughts and ideas on property investment and many who actively offer property on the newsfeeds of these sites.

Now you would think that this is an impossible task, to find a property investment in an arena full of people wanting to do the same but there are many posts which ask whether people have more deals than they can afford to fund and will therefore introduce opportunities to others, sometimes in return for a fee. Now remember there is no excuse for not undertaking the normal due diligence on any of these deals but it is another avenue which may yield you a positive result.

If you agree with the above about social media then you must appreciate the value in networking and talking to real people. If I think back over the last few properties I have purchased it looks like this: 1 via public auction, 1 from an agent who called me before a property came to the market, 1 from an agent who called me the day a property was listed on the market and 1 from an agent who called me and said he had a property which had been on the market for several months and that the owner would consider an offer significantly below the asking price. For this last one I agreed at 25% below the asking price. Talk to people, get to know people and little by little the calls will start to come in to you.

One marketing initiative I am not going to suggest is what the industry calls bandit boards. It works on the basis that people erect boards stating that they want a property in a particular development or location. Alternatively they place posters or other advertising at railway stations, telephone kiosks and the like. I do not recommend these methods as they are all likely to be unlawful. The issue of agent style boards is covered by the 1987 Town and Country Planning (Control of Advertisements) Act and you should further be aware that many leases prohibit the erection of any boards or advertising whatsoever or restrict it to the advertising only for sale or to let of a property within that development.

If you are going to make property your career you do not want to be caught meandering over the line of good practice and legality.

As well as developing a business and your power team it is important to remember to also develop yourself! There is no shortage of weekend courses on property investment available however I have never attended one and therefore am loathed to state an opinion on the merits of the educational experience they provide. My initial thoughts are that you would possibly gain more from a course which is strictly educational rather than one that is run by one of the property sourcing groups which may have the end goal of selling you one of their properties.

Additionally or alternatively you may wish to join one of the accreditation schemes. They normally involve a one-day course with a test at the end and are well worth doing. Some years ago, I attended the Kent one and despite having been in the industry for over 10 years and having a number of qualifications relating to property, I can confirm I learned something new as well as having the opportunity to meet some very interesting people. A quick check on the Internet should highlight a course near you.

A particular benefit of these accreditation courses is that they may give you discounts with your local authority on licensing fees. Contact your local council and see what they do in your area. Again you may find that the savings more than outweigh the cost of the course.

Further, In order to keep oneself up to date it may be prudent to consider joining one of the landlord organisations and there is likely to be one in your area. Aside from keeping your knowledge up to date it will also give you the chance to network with similar minded individuals.

An additional advantage is that some of the landlord associations have offers for landlords based on their bulk buying capabilities. I should declare an interest here as my firm provide a tenant eviction service to a number of these landlord associations! The savings can far outweigh any membership costs so it's certainly worth looking into.

You may even wish to undertake some relevant qualifications. If this is the case you could consider the examinations of the Association of Residential Letting Agents or the Certificate in Residential Lettings and Management which I believe is run by the National Federation of Property Professionals.

The more you speak to like minded people the better the connections and knowledge you will develop. There is absolutely no downside to increasing your knowledge and skills.

CHAPTER 10
GOT THIS FAR, WHAT COULD GO WRONG?

Do not be embarrassed by your failures, learn from them and start again.
Richard Branson.

It is a very common misconception that life as a property investor is an easy life. You simply collect rent from your tenants and then once you have had enough you sell the property for far more than you bought it for and pocket even more money.

For those readers who still hope this to be the position, you are in for a huge disappointment! The life of a landlord is challenging and has become far more so over the last few years.

Quite aside from the efforts of acquiring and managing your property, there are reams of legislation which directly impact the landlord and whilst it is not within the brief of this book to detail all of them, I feel it appropriate to give you a flavour of the legislative issues that you should consider if you are entering a career in the world of property investing.

Houses in Multiple Occupation:

Historically it was popular to split houses into separate rooms and collect more rent from an assortment of different individuals. There has certainly been a resurgence in this given the population of students, migrants and young professionals and the ever increasing rent levels particularly in some of the major cities throughout the UK.

To undertake this type of letting nowadays requires incredible organisation and administration skills. Initially the property will need to be licensed by the local authority. They will detail how many people can reside there and ensure things like fire precautions and the like are up to scratch. Many local authorities are reluctant to grant new HMO licences and so of this is something you are keen on then make sure you do some due diligence before committing to purchase the property.

The landlord is likely to expend a significant sum to get the property ready, licensed and tenanted, all which must happen before the property earns you a penny. Once let, landlords should be aware that his type of accommodation provides for the highest level of tenant turnover and probably the highest level of arrears of rent and definitely the highest level of wear and tear. All of these issues will impact the net yield that your investment can give you.

Another point worth noting is that some HMO landlords include the utilities within the rent. I have long argued that this is a false economy. The better option is to install a metering system.

Firstly it is illegal to try and sell gas, electricity and the like at a premium to your tenants and so there is no scope of a profit on this aspect of the money the tenant pays. Secondly and more importantly it is my experience that if you are paying your heating bill yourself then when it gets cold you would close the windows, put a jumper on and then perhaps put the heating on. You would turn the heating off once the house was warm.

Makes sense right? If you are not paying the bills then when it gets cold the heating goes on full and when it warms up the windows get opened but the heating remains on.

If you don't believe me then consider why your children leave their lights, TV and games console on and whilst dressed in T-shirt and shorts, turn the heating thermostat up because they are cold. I am adamant my son Ben will use far less electricity when he leaves home - for the sole reason that he will have to start paying for it!

The other issue with some HMO projects is the type of tenant that they attract. Whilst many HMOs are ideal for working professionals, transient workers and the like, many are used by local authorities to house those with issues that could potentially cause the landlord a headache.

This in itself can carry some dangers given that these people are also generally not financially self-sufficient. If for example their housing benefit claim is cancelled or the amount paid is reduced this could have a direct impact on the landlords cash flow. It's for these reasons that I would personally only accept an application from a housing benefit applicant where the application is supported by a suitable guarantor.

HMOs are very much on the legislative radar and landlords should therefore be alert to how changes and proposals could impact them.

One example of this is the changes that occurred with residential care homes where the minimum room sizes were changed and in a pen stroke rendered many care homes redundant. Whilst local authorities may have room standards currently how would your building fare if these were changed? These considerations should form part of your due diligence process.

Landlords should bear in mind that they can be heavily fined for failing to hold an HMO licence where one is required or fined if they do not comply with the terms of that licence. In addition, in the event that the landlord fails to obtain the licence the tenants can make an application to have their rent paid back to them.

Selective licensing:

The 2004 Housing Act also made provision for the introduction of areas of selective licensing and it is something that many of the local authorities have now introduced with many more considering their implementation. Basically the authority propose an area within their borough, or in some cases the whole borough, where the licensing will be implemented. Landlords with property in those areas are then required to obtain a licence for each and every property they have in that area. The costs are typically around £500 per property. The licence application requires the landlord to submit gas certificates, electrical certificates, floor plans and often a fire risk assessment in order that the landlords application be considered.

Minimum Property Sizes:

Someone recently asked me the minimum size a flat needed to be in my area. The answer is 30 square metres but it got me thinking. What if an investor had 10 flats this size and then the regulations changed. Would they be retrospective and if so what would that do to the investors portfolio?

My personal view is that you should aim to acquire property which provides a sensible level of accommodation. Not only will it make for a happier tenant but it will probably mean they rent from you for longer and the capital appreciation could be far better than that achieved with a very small flat.

Energy Performance Certificates:

Many landlords and many more prospective property investors are still unaware that there is an obligation to provide an energy performance certificate for all tenancies created or renewed since 2007. The certificate, which costs around £50, details the energy efficiency of the property and makes suggestions in terms of how these can be improved. Just another piece of paper to provide to the tenant you may think, but do you also know that very soon there is likely to be a complete ban on landlords letting properties that have and F or a G rating? Furthermore there is to be an obligation placed on landlords to comply with any reasonable request made by their tenant to improve the energy efficiency of the building.

Landlords should therefore consider the property they are thinking of buying and pay particular attention to the EPC rating not because they are paying the bills but because of the exponential costs they could incur in the future as this and other legislation makes its way on to the statute books.

Housing Benefit Rates:

Many landlords are really feeling the pinch given that the level of housing benefit, known now as the local housing allowance, has generally been reduced as part of the nations austerity measures. Furthermore there is a proposal to introduce a scheme called Universal Credit where the tenant benefits are wrapped into one payment and given to the tenant direct. Many landlords have properties in areas where there is a high dependency on housing benefit and it becomes difficult to collect a figure greater than the local housing allowance. If you are considering purchasing a property which is likely to appeal to housing benefit tenants then you should give consideration to the level of the local housing allowance that is available.

To give you an example I have a client who purchased three terraced properties in town in the North East of England. The agent who sold them to him said that they would achieve £450 per month and gave him a guaranteed rent for 6 months. The reality was that the local housing allowance is in the region of £300 a month and that is all they are likely to achieve. The six month rent guarantee was in essence just a sellers inducement to get the properties sold. Once he had purchased them he was paid £450 per month for six months even though they sat empty and once a tenant was secured some 8 months after he had bought them the rent achieved was £300 a month. If you are considering housing benefit tenants then you must be aware of the local housing allowance rates. Otherwise you could be in for a rude awakening and the yield that your property will produce could be decimated.

The current housing benefit system creates a rent level which is supposed to allow access to the lowest priced third of available property on the market. You should be aware that this is set in advance and so in a rising market the level of LHA will look even less adequate than it may do in a falling or static rental market. The default position is that the council will pay the money to the tenant direct and then it is the job of the landlord to try and get the tenant to pay the rent. There are circumstances where the landlord can get the local authority to pay the rent direct to the landlord and whilst the circumstances under which the council will do so vary between each council there is an accepted position that the council will divert payments to the landlord in the event that the tenant falls eight or more weeks in arrears.

There are many misconceptions surrounding tenants who are in receipt of a benefit award and it is for the landlord to judge which is the best tenant for their particular property. Many landlords refuse to accept benefit tenants but this can mean that you can miss out on some super tenants. Consider the key worker who is on minimum wage but receives some state assistance, consider the retired single lady who is reliant solely on a state pension, or those who are in a temporary period of unemployment but who possess the skills which should mean they will very shortly find a new job.

My personal view is that I consider all on their merits. As a broad rule I will not be too taken by those who could work but refuse to or those who seem to think that the world owes them a living. In contrast I am normally very drawn to those who are trying against challenging circumstances or those who have had a genuine run of bad luck. Regardless of your viewpoint, you should consider that, to the best of my knowledge, there is no available statistical data which can confirm which type of tenant is more likely to maintain the property or cause damage to it.

The tenant profile you are looking for should be considered prior to purchase of the property. If you are not wanting tenants in receipt of a benefits award then there are some locations and streets that you should avoid as it will be very hard to find a private tenant. Again it is all part of the due diligence process.

Council Tax:

Recently many local authorities have changed the way they deal with Council Tax meaning that you may have to pay the full council tax for any periods during which your property is vacant. You should be aware of this as it is an additional cost you may not have budgeted for and one which will arise at a period during which you are not receiving rent.

Personal Injury Claims:

Given the recent explosion in so called "ambulance chasing" personal injury firms there seems to be no shortage of law firms happy to act on a no win no fee basis to assist in all sorts of personal injury claims. Having been involved in the lettings industry for 20 years I can confirm that I had not even heard of a landlord being sued for personal injury before about 2009. Now it seems to be a far more common issue that landlords face.

In my experience the tenant is either approached by a personal injury firm to establish if they have ever had an accident or they are lured by the prospect of some cash by one of the numerous adverts that appear on TV and in the press. The personal injury firm then writes to the landlord notifying them of the alleged accident and asking them to notify their insurance company. Depending on the outcome, the result for the landlord could be an increased insurance premium.

It does however serve as a sobering reminder that the landlord owes their tenant a duty of care.

Gas and Electricity:

Landlords will no doubt be aware of the requirement to have a Gas Safe registered engineer check their gas appliances every twelve months but it may be useful to speak with your engineer to see what other requirements are being introduced.

One recent example is the changes to gas safety laws so that a carbon monoxide detector is now required in the event that the boiler flue passes through a room before it exits the building. Aside from the additional cost for the landlord they need to be aware of these changes to ensure that they are compliant.

It is recommended, although not a legislative requirement to have the electrical installation checked by a qualified electrician at least once in every five year period. Landlords should also be aware that any alterations to the electrical installation should be undertaken by someone suitably qualified.

Checking nationality and permission to be in the UK:
At time of writing there is a pilot scheme in the West Midlands area where it is now the landlord and agents obligation to ensure that the tenants they deal with have the right to live in the UK. The suggestion is that if sufficient checks are not made that there could be significant fines imposed on those who fall foul of the legislation. Assuming the pilot goes to plan the intention is that the scheme will be rolled out throughout the UK at some stage in 2015.

Not only do you need to check for your tenants but you need to check for all occupiers of the property. Their documents will need to be seen by you personally or alternatively via live video link and you should be able to confirm that they are original and have not been tampered with.

You will also need to keep the documents for at least 12 months following the end of the tenancy as the Home Office can ask to inspect them. Failing to comply will land you with a

£3000 fine so make sure you do some checks. For those of you nervous about fulfilling your obligations for this new legislation, there are a number of firms springing up who will undertake the checks for you.

Tenant eviction:
Another danger you may fall foul of is that of a bad tenant. There are around 170,000 applications each year from landlords wanting to remove their tenants from their property and so the incidence of a bad tenant is probably more common than you thought. Aside from the obvious breaches such as non-payment of rent there are other issues such as anti social behaviour, criminal activity to name but two.

My firm have acted for several landlords where their properties were being used to cultivate drugs, used as a brothel and I even sold a house a few years ago where the former owner had used the property as a printing press for producing counterfeit bank notes!

I have talked about the process of tenant eviction earlier in this book and so there is no merit in repeating myself but just be mindful that you must follow the legislative framework for dealing with problem tenants as the alternative will cause you, the landlord, problems.

Article 4:
There is a general permitted development order which allows for a number of things which may otherwise require planning permission. The Article 4 legislation makes some changes to this. The local authority can introduce an Article 4 declaration in certain areas which means that landlords may have to make planning applications for some things they may not need to in other areas. One in particular is often where a landlord wants to

convert a standard home into a property let to Students or let as rooms. Make sure you check with your local authority.

Fire risk:
There is legislation in place where a fire risk assessment should be undertaken for rented property in particular where there are any common or communal areas. The risk assessment is required to be kept and monitored and reviewed at regular intervals.

Legionella:
More recently legislation has been introduced to protect against legionella. Landlords need to have a risk assessment undertaken and should also ensure that a review system is in place to ensure that the risks are minimised.

Claims from landlords:
Investors who act as an agent for landlords should be alert to the fact that the landlord may claim against them. The Agent owes the landlord a duty of care and needs to act in the landlords best interests. Failure to do so may lead to a claim for damages based on negligence. Those who act as an agent must also be a member of one of the property redress schemes not least as failure to do so could leave you open to a significant fine.

I hope the previous paragraphs have given you some food for thought. The Landlords life is far from easy. In short I would suggest that if you are unsure of any of your obligations as a landlord then you should seek some professional advice.

CHAPTER 11
EXPLODING THE MYTHS.

I believe in everything until it's disproved. So I believe the myths. It all exists, even if it's in your mind.

John Lennon

There are a number of myths out there, which many landlords may be confused by. I will endeavour to address a number of them in the following pages.

1.
The first myth I want to deal with is the one that states that by investing in property you can become a millionaire in 12 months.

Without wanting to disappoint you too greatly, this is incredibly unlikely to happen for two reasons. Firstly if you are investing, then even if you created an equity value of £1M those funds would be tied up in your properties and to try and release them would increase your debt pile and therefore eat into the income that the property generates by way of increased mortgage payments.

Furthermore you are most unlikely to be able to create £1M equity within a year. Most investors consider themselves happy if they manage to buy a property at 20% below what they feel it could achieve on the open market. Let us be generous and assume that once they own it they can improve value and so have a total of 30% equity. On this basis you would have to invest over £3M and within 12 months create 30% uplift on each and every property to create £1M in a year.

What is more likely to be achievable is the creation of a portfolio valued at £1M in 12 months. Hard to do from a standing start, but certainly possible. However bear in mind that this may not be your game plan, as it would mean having significant mortgage payments to meet.

My view with property investment has long been that it can be a good alternative to a pension scheme and can provide a steady and reasonably regular return. Those who plan to get rich quickly are often left very disappointed.

2.
The other most common one I hear is that being a Buy to Let landlord is easy!
Again I would contest that this is not the case. Ask any property manager at your local letting agency whether property management is a doddle and you will get only one answer! Buy to let is far from easy. Aside from dealing with property issues you have to deal with the issues of tenants. People display different personalities and characteristics and so there is no pre-set formula to either the things that tenants will do or the way they will respond to the landlords actions. It is important to bear in mind that property management is a people business and should therefore never be described as easy!

To follow are some other myths and misconceptions that I have heard over the years together with my personal thoughts on them.

3.

Below Market Value:

There has been almost an industry established on the basis of Below Market Value Property (BMV). I find this rather remarkable.

The view that there are sellers out there who will agree to sell their property for up to 25% less than it is "worth" appears to me to be incredible. To adopt an example lets say that you are offered a property for £75,000, which is reportedly worth £100,000 and comes with a "valuation" to support that higher figure.

If you enquire why the property is discounted you will be told that the seller is keen to sell as they are struggling with their mortgage, getting divorced, emigrating etc etc. and that there is therefore a need for a swift sale.

If it is a quick and certain sale that they require then why was the property not sold at auction. If it were truly worth £100,000 then it would most likely achieve around that figure if it were sold at public auction. If it were a divorce situation then the sellers would want the most they can from the situation, if someone was emigrating then they would want as much as they can get to start their new life elsewhere and if someone was struggling with their mortgage they would want the most they can to maximise their chance of paying off the mortgage or dealing with any mortgage arrears.

My view is therefore that the property is most likely worth around £75,000 rather than £100,000. That being the case why would an investor pay a fee to a property sourcer for finding a property on the market at market value. You could do that yourself!

This is not to say that property cannot be bought below its true value by using your situation to your advantage. Buyers can sometimes negotiate a great purchase price on the basis that they are a cash buyer, or will move quickly, or will pay a non returnable deposit, or don't require a survey etc. but these negotiating tools are to be used on each purchase and cannot generally be used in the event that you are using a property sourcer as any discount will potentially eat into their fee.

I have never used a property sourcer and never would do. Whilst I am not so arrogant to think that no one in my market place is more expert than myself, what I am certain of is that no one will be more careful with my money than I would be. To illustrate this point look at some of the uses of money which are made by local authorities and the Government. There are regularly allegations of huge wastes of money and if you consider that the people concerned were spending their own money, is it not fair to say there would be far less wastage and far more consideration before funds are committed to something? I rest my case.

More specifically in relation to property, a sourcer will charge a fee from you for acquiring the property. In the event that they cannot find a property that fits your requirements then, unless you have arranged for a retainer, they won't earn any money. For that reason it is unlikely that they will report that there is nothing suitable available at a given time. In such circumstances they will possibly suggest you purchase the best of a bad bunch so that they get their fee.

4.

Guaranteed Rent Schemes:

There have been a number of property sourcers and property clubs who have sourced investments where the rent is guaranteed at a certain level for say the first 12 months. When considering this level of income the property purchase price looks good and it is quite possible that in using these numbers, an investment could fit the triangle.

What you should bear in mind is that in my view, the rent guaranteed will almost certainly be far higher than the market can support and the difference between the rent achievable and the rent promised is just an inducement by the seller to justify the purchase price.

I looked after a property for a Client who purchased a property for £180,000 in a coastal town. It was a lovely 2 bedroom flat and situated in a block in which I looked after several others.

He was told that he was getting the property at a 25% discount to market value and was shown a valuation proving this to be the case. In addition to believing the property was worth in excess of a quarter of a million pounds he was informed that the rent was guaranteed at £1000 per month. As a result the property would fit in the triangle for an investor looking for a gross yield in excess of 6%.

The reality is that the other flats in the block sold without a 25% discount at between £150,000 and £160,000 and the best rent that any of the flats has achieved is £600 per month.

The developer, by offering a £6,000 rent enhancement, has managed to get an additional £25,000 profit on the flat.

The purchaser has an immediate deficit of £25,000, a property which will yield him 4% and had to pay a £6,000 fee to the property club for the privilege.

Do not be blind to this scam. Rental values are easily accessible and you should not sway from your view of what a property could achieve just because the seller will guarantee it at a different level for a year. If you are still unsure then remember that a good letting agent will be able to provide you with some comparable rental data to enable you to make an informed decision.

5.
Off plan Purchasing:
I have yet to see a new build off plan scheme which will realistically work with the property triangle. Generally, new builds attract a premium of around 10% against their second hand counterparts and yet the rental income (aside from perhaps the first let when the place is brand new) will rarely be any higher.

In fact I have seen a number of cases where second hand stock gets a higher rental, as the room sizes are often bigger.

Notwithstanding, developers often offer packages to Buy to Let Investors citing how suited their new build property is to property investment.

Whilst I cannot say that new build will never fit with the property triangle I do urge you to use the triangle to assess how viable a new build purchase could be.

A further word of caution when it comes to new build property is to exercise extreme caution if buying an "investment" deal from a developer. Let's say there is a development of 50 flats and that 40 of them are bought by investors on the basis that the rent is "guaranteed" for a year.

At the end of that year the investors may realise that the rent they are likely to get on an ongoing basis is less and therefore they may decide to sell the property and buy something that will give them a greater yield. All sounds fine but what if all 40 of those Buy to Let flats come to the sales market at the end of the initial 12 months. All are the same and so unless yours is the cheapest then you are likely to have to wait until the other 39 flats sell. The result will no doubt be that there will be some hard bargaining on price and you may well have to sell at a loss to get out. It is only with such new build sites that the situation of mass sale at the same time can potentially occur. It is a risk that I would always avoid.

6.
New Build Apartments are the way to go:
Many people will tell you that new build offer a superb choice for the buy to let investor. Indeed many of the property clubs, which popped up in the 1990s, championed new build apartments to their investors. This theory is flawed for a variety of reasons. Firstly there is invariably a "new build premium" attached to the price of a new build unit. They are generally more expensive than a comparable second hand house partly due to the existence of a builder's warranty and partly due to some of the incentives the developer offers which have to be paid for by someone. This premium is generally evidenced if you research the resale prices of new build homes after a couple of years.

To those landlords who say that because everything is new there will be no repairs or renewals required, I disagree. The things, which require attention in a property throughout a tenancy, are partly due to wear and tear but partly due to the behaviour of a tenant. If the tenant chops their vegetables on your laminate worktop without a chopping board then the worktop will get ruined. Whether the worktop was brand new or 5 years old – the worktop will be ruined. Similarly the tenant is no more likely to burn a carpet with an iron or spill a glass of red wine if the carpet is brand new or 3 years old. The cost of replacement is the same and the likelihood of needing to replace is the same. I will however grant some credence to the argument that a tenant is more likely to look after a property that is decoratively immaculate than one that is decoratively tired but I will counter that with the argument that you are far less likely to recover money for damage to a property that was poor quality at the start. However you package it up an investor should be very careful if they want to consider new build as part of a Buy to let investment strategy.

A further risk with a new build scheme is that there is likely to be an element of social housing within the development although at the time you purchase your unit it may not be clear who is going to occupy these properties. Furthermore you have no idea whether the entire development will be sold to Buy to let investors and if this turns out to be the case there is less chance that gardens and exteriors will be well maintained and this could place downward pressure on values.

A further issue for the investor wanting to consider new build is the financing of it. Many lenders were very badly hurt in the last 10 years or so by inflated values, guaranteed rents and the like and as a result some lenders will refuse to entertain the purchase of new build apartments on a Buy to let basis. My view remains that the property investor could do better with second hand stock rather than new. Indeed run the figures through the property triangle and you will see.

7.
Overseas and Holiday lettings:
Regardless of what you may think, Holiday letting is a significantly different offering than standard letting. Aside from the increased wear and tear to the property and shorter period of lettings there are also a far higher incidence of voids and a huge variation in the rent achievable during the course of the year. As a result you should take a very different view of yields if this is an investment you are considering.

To give you an example let us say that we have a two bedroom sea facing apartment in a coastal town which has a standard rent of £900 a month. This could realistically achieve £10,000 a year for a standard letting. If the property was used as a holiday let the landlord would have to furnish it to a reasonable standard and in all likelihood have an ongoing advertising spend to continue to attract people to use it for their holidays.

Generally speaking the property could be let at a reasonable rent of say £750 a week for the Christmas, Easter and Summer school holiday periods which could give an income of around £7500 but it could be rather hit and miss to try and get the property filled during the balance of the year. On this basis the property could achieve say £7500 to £8000 per annum as a holiday let but require at least 10 visits to check in and check out people, launder bedding, clean, repair or replace broken or damaged furniture, ongoing advertising and council tax for the period that the property is vacant. You also run the risk of receiving a booking from the single male who wants the property for a few days only for you to subsequently find out your property was hosting 10 lads for a stag party. You will probably also find that the property insurance will be more expensive given that the property could be empty for more than 30 days at a time. So actually you may be better off with a standard let.

For the above reason you should be incredibly sceptical of offers of holiday lets where the seller states that a 15% yield is achievable. This may be the case for one week of the year, may be based on an unrealistic occupancy rate and regardless of the truth of those claims, the picture could be incredibly different if you calculate the net costs and therefore the net yield.

The situation can become even more precarious if you consider overseas property. This so called "Jet to Let" is not for the faint hearted not only due to a different legislative framework, the difficulty for non-nationals to enforce covenants and many peculiar by-laws. Did you know that in some countries you cannot evict a tenant in the Winter whilst in others if a tenant is granted a tenancy of over a year they are entitled to stay for many more? Without knowledge of local legislation you are far more likely to come unstuck. My advice is that if you are looking to invest in property then start in a country and area that you know and where you understand the customs and cultures of the people who are likely to want to rent your property.

8.
Repossessions are cheap:
My experience with repossessions is that they are rarely cheap. There is a fundamental reason why this is the case. Repossessions are handled by LPA Receivers and Banks and not by the seller and therefore the emotional part of the transaction does not exist. It is purely a commercial transaction. Additionally there is an obligation for the seller to

get as much money for the property as is possible so as to avoid facing any litigation from the defaulting borrower that the property was undersold.

As such the bank will offer the property for sale and continue marketing it right up until the time contracts are exchanged. They will generally accept a higher offer even if a sale is already agreed. Contrary to what you may have read they are not normally hugely incentivised to get the property sold very quickly at any price. Instead they will insist on a full marketing campaign to get the highest amount of money.

In my opinion you are more likely to get a "deal" when purchasing property by focussing your attentions on a motivated individual vendor rather than a corporate one.

9.
Private sellers negotiate harder as they don't even want to pay an estate agents fee:
This is another myth in my opinion. Not only do private sellers generally have a lesser response due to more restricted marketing than those who use a good estate agent but private sellers generally have less skill in negotiation and even where they do it is a fact that people can negotiate better for a third party than they can for themselves.

For those reading this who disagree, consider why therefore professional footballers have an agent who negotiates their terms and conditions, why pop stars have an agent and indeed why over 90% of property sellers are represented by an agent.

If you think you can beat these odds then consider the following. If you wanted a pay rise do you think you could get a better pay deal by speaking directly with your firms Senior

Management or if your Line Manager negotiated on your behalf? Having been in this situation before I can confirm that I have procured better pay rises for my staff than I ever negotiated for myself!

In my view private sellers offer, in some circumstances, a property investor the opportunity to negotiate a good deal.

10.
Auction property is sold cheaply:
Again this is to me a myth. Whilst I appreciate that some property is offered at auction with a no or low reserve and some auctions are poorly attended which means the investor can bag a deal, this is far from the norm.

Indeed the more normal course of events is that the property is entered into an auction and in the three weeks before the sale almost every quality investor buyer who invests in that area will have a look at it with a view to bidding. Given that as soon as the hammer falls the property is sold, some buyers will get caught up emotionally in the bidding and pay a little more than perhaps they wanted to on the basis that they do not want to go home empty handed. Far from a location to source a bargain an auction house can be the complete opposite.

Generally too, auction lots go through thorough nationwide advertising to attract a wide pool of buyers and some of the bigger auction house mailing lists run to around 50,000 buyers. On this basis you would have less competition and possibly more chance of a deal if you received a call from a friendly estate agent stating that they had a property coming to the market and did you want to see it before it hits the market.

I have bought property at auction and will continue to do so however I always set myself a ceiling and if someone wants to pay more than me then I let them. It is as simple as that.

11.
Planning permission is easy to obtain.

Many property investors look at property on the basis that they can purchase the property, add a planning permission and procure a profit. I agree it can be done but planning permissions, consents for change of use, subdivision, and building in back gardens are far from foregone conclusions. Engage an architect or as an absolute minimum talk to the local authority before you commit to purchase. A couple of hundred pounds on pre planning advice could be the difference between success and a very costly mistake.

12.
Tenants rarely misbehave:

As I have mentioned earlier, there are almost 200,000 applications to courts each year to evict tenants. Your business model should factor in for some arrears of rents, some repair and replacements and a void period. If you work on the basis of 100% occupancy then you are likely to be disappointed.

CONCLUSION.

When you have a dream that you can't let go of, trust your instincts and pursue it. But remember: Real dreams take work, they take patience, and sometimes they require you to dig down very deep. Be sure you're willing to do that.
Harvey Mackay

It is almost with some sadness that I approach the end of this my first book. I have thoroughly enjoyed reflecting on my experiences and sharing my thoughts and ideas with you even though we have yet to meet!

I hope that you now have a confidence to invest in property given that you are now equipped to source property, equipped to value property, equipped to make an offer on a property and equipped to progress that offer through to exchange and completion. In addition you also now have an insight into the subsequent sale or letting of your investment.

Furthermore there were hopefully some pearls of wisdom within these pages which will ensure that you steer clear of some of the more common mistakes that some investors make and to be aware of some of the urban myths surrounding property investment.

I genuinely hope that you feel that you have learned something new from my book and that you can approach your property investment journey with a greater confidence and hopefully enormous enthusiasm.

If you were a novice investor at the start of this book I hope I have given you some ideas, some support and the confidence to go out there and make it happen. Whilst you will never stop learning I hope I have given you enough information in these pages to avoid you making any serious mistakes.

If you were a seasoned operator at the start of this book, I trust there was at least something which you found useful, thought provoking or interesting contained within the preceding pages.

As my experience will testify, property investment it is a lifelong learning curve and hopefully a continually enjoyable one. You will always be able to learn something new and for that reason I heartily recommend you network with like minded people and share their skills, experience and knowledge. Perhaps you have some friends who are also investing in property or alternatively you may want to attend one of the many landlord networking events that are held around the country. A quick Internet search should reveal the one nearest to you.

For those of you who have any specific questions, either relating to the content of my book or around the wider sphere of property investment, I invite you to contact me. I would be delighted to hear from you and pleased to be able to assist you if I can.

To all of you, I thank you sincerely for taking the time to read my book and may I take this opportunity to wish you well on your property journey. May it be fruitful, lucrative, successful, rewarding and above all enjoyable.

Build on your new found knowledge and confidence by getting started on your journey of property investment straight away. I don't want you to be the person who *sees* the opportunity but rather the person who will *seize* the opportunity!

Finally, it would be great if you would provide me with some feedback in terms of what you thought of my book and what you feel you have learned.

I can be contacted via email at graham@grahamkinnear.com

Kind regards,

Graham.

Graham Kinnear BSc (Hons), FPCS, CPEA, CRLM, MGIS, CeMAP, FPC, MLIA (Dip), DipDEA.

GLOSSARY:

Accreditation:
The process by which a landlord obtains an approved qualification from a recognised body.

Air bricks:
Brick shaped ventilation blocks used to provide ventilation and air flow beneath a timber floor.

Angel investor:
The input of funds by a third party private individual or company in anticipation of a financial return.

Annuities:
The financial product generally purchased to provide an income in retirement.

Article 4:
A piece of legislation implemented by a local authority which means that certain changes of use of a property will still require the consent of the local authority despite the relaxation of planning rules.

BMV (Below market value):
A concept which has had plenty of media coverage and signifying property which is being offered at a figure below what it is apparently worth in the market place.

Caveat emptor:
Let the Buyer beware

Ceiling price:
A description used to describe the highest property price that can be sustained in a given street or location.

Chancel search:
A search of data to establish whether there is a liability to contribute to parish costs.

Client:
The person who pays the provider for their goods or services

Cold start office:
An office which has not previously traded or existed in a given location.

Commission:
The element of pay received by an individual which is dependent upon his or her performance.

Completion:
The legal explanation of once a property transaction has finished in that the seller has the financial proceeds of the sale and the buyer has the property.

Consumer unit:
The device which was historically referred to as fuse board. The unit which holds the various circuit devices for the property electrical supply.

Conveyance:
The process of transferring the legal title of a property from the seller to the buyer.

Domestic energy surveyor:
A qualified individual able to undertake an energy performance survey to calculate the energy efficiency of a property.

EDC:
The initials for Exchange with delayed completion. Where the purchaser exchanges on a property but may not, with the agreement of the seller, complete the transaction for say a year or more.

Equitable interest:
The financial calculation of market value minus outstanding mortgage/loans.

Exchange of contracts:
The point at which the buyer is obliged to buy and the seller is obliged to sell. The point at which either side would face penalty in the event that they pulled out of the transaction.

Fixtures and Fittings Form:
The standard form provided to property sellers in which they details the fixtures and fittings that are to be included in the sale or available by separate negotiation.

Freehold:
The form of legal title which describes the owner as owning the property as well as the land it is situate upon.

Gas Safety Certificate:
The certificate produced following an inspection by a Gas Safe approved gas engineer of a boiler and any gas appliance. These are required annually for tenanted residential properties.

Gearing:
The use of borrowed money to increase purchasing power.

Government redress scheme:
A scheme recently introduced which requires anyone acting in the capacity of an agent to register with one of the three approved redress schemes.

Ground rent:
The amount required under the terms of a lease to be paid to the freeholder. This is normally an annual charge of between nil and £250 per year

HMO:
The abbreviation for House of Multiple Occupation.

Housing benefit/housing allowance:
The state assistance provided to individuals to assist with the payment of their rent.

Inflation:
The increase in costs, also known as the retail price index.

Jv partner:
Abbreviation for Joint Venture partner and describes the purchase of a property using funds pooled from two or more people as a collective investment

Landlords clinic:
A question and answer session held at landlord networking events.

Lease:
The document which describes the terms and conditions under which someone is entitled to occupy land or property.

Leasehold:
The legal title which confers the right to occupy for a term of years. Different to freehold the owner of the lease does not own the land upon which the property is situated.

Lease option:
Term used to describe an agreement where someone has a lease of a building with the inbuilt ability that they can purchase that property for a predetermined amount at some stage in the future.

Leverage:
See gearing

Liquid investment:
The liquidity of an investment refers to the ease at which it can be converted to cash. Stocks and shares are relatively liquid, property is less so.

Local housing allowance:
The current term for housing benefit payments which are paid on behalf of tenants with low or no incomes in order to assist with their housing costs.

Local search:
The enquiries that are undertaken as part of a property purchase to see if the property is likely to be affected by proposed road works, restrictions or other changes of which the local council could be aware.

LPA Receiver:
The LPA stands for Law of Property Act and the LPA receiver is someone normally appointed by a finance company to manage the asset upon which their money is secured upon. Normally appointed when the borrower has got themselves into difficulty.

Margin call:
Where the value of the property has fallen so that the percentage of the loan compared to the property value has breached the percentage agreed with the bank. In such circumstances the bank may ask for a payment to get the percentage back to within agreed limits. Such payment request is a margin call.

Marriage value:
The additional value generated when an enfranchising leaseholder owns both the leasehold and freehold estates.

Memorandum of sale:
The document normally issued by the estate agent showing the proposed buyer and seller of a property together with the solicitors each are using and the price that has been agreed for the property.

National savings:
Savings functions provided by the Government and promoted by the Post Office.

Networking:
The meeting and connecting with like minded people with a view to assisting each other in their respective goals.

Off Plan:
The description of a property purchase where the property has not yet been built. Normally where the buyer selects the plot they will buy from the architects' plans.

Passive income:
An income that occurs without the person physically working for it. Rental income is often considered passive income.

Pension:
The financial vehicle to provide you with an income once you have stopped working due to your age.

Property information form:
A standard form which is provided to the seller of a property sale to complete. It includes details of boundaries, services connected and the like with the aim to provide the buyer with more information on the property they are considering purchasing

Proxy bid:
The submission of a bid prior to an auction with the instruction that the auctioneer will bid up to that figure on your behalf.

Recession:
The contracting of the economy for two or more consecutive quarter periods.

Rent Acts:
Principally refers to the 1977 Act under which tenancies were created before the legislation changed and permitted the assured shorthold tenancy

Rent to rent:
The method of property investment where someone lets a property either for or from a landlord and then sublets it at a greater amount with the difference being their income.

Repossession:
Generally the sale of a property by a bank or building society who is in control of a property as a result of the borrower defaulting on the terms of a loan secured on the property.

Residual valuation:
A calculation of a property value by taking its end value and then deducting any costs which will be incurred in getting it to its end value Often used to value land or properties in need of refurbishment.

Reversionary Value:
The value of the property once the lease has expired

Selective licensing:
A licensing scheme permitted by the 2004 Housing Act which allows the Local authority to charge a fee to administer their scheme with the aim of improving standards and landlord behaviour in a certain area.

Service charge:
The charge made by a freeholder to the leaseholder in respect of the costs they incur in maintaining and insuring a property. The lease of the property should detail what items the service charge can include.

SPV:
The abbreviation of Special Purchase Vehicle and typically refers to a limited liability company set up for the sole purpose of owning a property or properties.

Venture capital:
Capital from third party investors who require a return. Funding is normally for far shorter periods than is the case with mortgage funding.

Yield:
Gross yield is the calculation of annual rent divided by purchase price. It is generally presented as a percentage.

Printed in Great Britain
by Amazon